THE PARTY THAT LASTED IOO DAYS

THE PARTY THAT LASTED 100 DAYS

The Late Victorian Season: A Social Study

Hilary and Mary Evans

MACDONALD AND JANE'S · LONDON

*The illustrations are all from the collection of
the Mary Evans Picture Library, London. The following abbreviations have
been used in the captions:*

*Cassells = Cassells Family Magazine
Doré, London = Doré and Jerrold, London: A Pilgrimage
ILN = Illustrated London News*

First published in Great Britain in 1976 by
Macdonald and Jane's Publishers Ltd.
Paulton House
8 Shepherdess Walk
City Road
London N1 7LW

Filmset and printed in Great Britain by
BAS Printers Limited, Wallop, Hampshire

ISBN 0 356 08363 2

Contents

Introduction:
YOUNG BARBARIANS
ALL AT PLAY

Anyone who delves back into the social life of nineteenth-century England sooner or later comes upon references to 'the Season'. But these references are nearly always oblique; it is taken for granted that the reader knows what the Season was, when it occurred, who took part in it and why.

Indeed, there was a time when this knowledge could be taken for granted. Even today, most of us have a vague notion of what the Season was all about, and for most purposes a vague notion is all we need. And yet the Season repays closer examination. It was a phenomenon in its own right, uniquely characteristic of the society which created it and uniquely informative about the relationships between one part of that society and another. For that matter, it can also be seen as a striking manifestation of a civilised community at a critical transitional stage in its development.

Because nothing like a complete account of the Season seems ever to have been published, this book is primarily a work of reconstruction. I have had to re-build the London Season item by item, picking up details from magazine articles, handbooks and personal memoirs. All the information is authentic in that it is first-hand; at the same time, it is unreliable for the same reason. But I found little or no contradiction; the pieces of the jigsaw fit quite comfortably, and I feel satisfied that the overall picture is a fair approximation of what the Season was really like.

And that, in the end, is what matters most. The details are picturesque and entertaining, and give the picture verisimilitude; but my first aim has been to try to understand *why* the London Season was so important to those to whom it seemed important. For the great majority of people, the Season was of no consequence; for a few, nothing in life mattered so much. Why?

We all require some stable elements in our lives—some continuity that will reassure us when everything else is in flux. For most of us this requirement is met by the necessity to earn our living; work imposes on us at least a routine, more often an absolute way of life which gives us if anything too much stability, too unbroken a continuity.

But there are certain classes of humanity who do not need to earn their living—who are either born free, or acquire freedom, or have it bequeathed to them in the

I

form of a country house, a home in Belgravia, a parcel of annual rents and a packet of sound bonds. There are, for instance, savage tribes who even in the twentieth century do not have to work (as we understand it) in order to stay alive: a little farming, a little hunting, and their needs are taken care of. And what do they do? They voluntarily limit their freedom by filling up their leisure hours with time-consuming rituals and ceremonies, hedging themselves around with sanctions and taboos, restricting their liberty with elaborately regulated etiquette.

Much the same is true of another leisured class—the rich. By 'rich' I do not mean people who have found a way of life which brings them in an income above the average; I mean people who have the use of a wealth far greater than any income derived from work could bring. Such wealth not only relieves them from the necessity of work, but allows them to choose what they will do with their leisure.

And what do they do? Like the savages, they seem to be afflicted by a kind of psychological agoraphobia. Take, for example, the French aristocracy in the age of Louis XIV; at the Court of Versailles they created what was perhaps the most artificial society the world has ever seen, in which the basic functions of eating, social intercourse, copulation and so forth were elaborated into baroque behaviour-patterns of unbelievable intricacy.

At that time, France was the world's 'top country', and it could be that this has something to do with the matter. For at the end of the nineteenth century it was England which had taken the lead; and it is in England that we find a comparable example of a social system created, quite artificially, by a leisured class for its own ends.

There were of course vast differences between the France of Louis XIV and the England of Victoria. France had been ruled by a more or less absolute monarch; England was constitutionally a democracy—and to a large extent was even one in practice. Both societies had their 'establishment', but the Victorian aristocracy, though involved and interconnected with the court, was not synonymous with it as the aristocracy of Versailles had been. English 'society', like the French aristocracy, was a wealthy and powerful élite, able to have its way in most matters, wallowing in privileges voluntarily accorded them by the majority of their fellow-countrymen. A few of its members earned their right to those privileges as conscientious leaders of the community, working hard as statesmen or busying themselves with specific areas of activity such as agricultural improvement or factory reform. But they were very much the minority. Of the majority, the best that can be said is that they generally did less harm than good. As components in the social machine they were superfluous.

The French aristocrats created the court of Versailles; the top people of England created the London Season. Once created, it kept itself going. There were some who stood back and marvelled, like Frankenstein, at the monster they had created. Charles Eyre Pascoe, who wrote his useful annual guide to the Season from the inside, seems to have had his fill by the time he prepared his 1903 edition of *London of Today*:

> Three weeks of the London Season are more than enough for anyone who works through the pleasures of the town with ordinary zeal and perseverance. When you have eaten half-a-dozen dinners at friends' houses, you will find that you have to decline a full dozen more. When you have fought your way through the barricades of humanity to the hostess at one grand dance, you will find you have no life left in you to struggle that way any more. When you have done one July reception, you will wish yourself on the moors. When you have done two, you will wish yourself at the bottom of the sea.

A garden party at Holland House. ILN, *1872*

But even those who complained continued to go along with it; the bandwagon had generated too much impetus for anything to halt it. Anything short of a world war, that is; and even then it took two such wars really to do the job. Indeed, even today its last vestiges can be seen at Ascot and Henley, quaint survivals of past splendours.

How was the Season able to acquire this impetus? In part, as I have already suggested, because the leisured society needed this kind of ritual defence against the emptiness of unlimited leisure. More overtly, there was the fact that the Season did indeed meet some practical requirements. It gave mothers a magnificent chance

3

to find husbands for their daughters and wives for their sons, for instance—though it is true that other sections of society managed to achieve those ends without going to quite so much trouble.

As to how each item on the Season's annual programme came to acquire its cult status, I think the obvious explanation is the correct one. The simple logical sequence—'in' people go to Henley; 'everybody' wants to be thought 'in'; so 'everybody' goes to Henley—is, I think, perfectly adequate as an explanation of the mechanism which operated, though precisely why the 'in' people made their selections in the first place is another matter. So, of course, is the question of why 'everybody'—or at any rate a substantial number of people—wanted to be 'in'; but that is a question of herd behaviour which would take us too far from the subject in hand. All we need do is register the fact that, of all those thousands who attended the Eton *v.* Harrow cricket match in the 1890s, the vast majority couldn't give a damn about cricket and couldn't care less which team won; but they would have been acutely miserable if anything had prevented them from attending the match.

And so the process continued, and in continuing acquired strength. Each additional acquiescence gave the ceremony more drawing-power to attract the

*Eton
v. Harrow
at Lord's.
Du Maurier,
Graphic,
1871*

acquiescence of another; and so more and more joined the herd, until at last for one reason or another the bubble burst (a popular restaurant becomes *too* popular, there isn't room, the 'in' people stop going, everyone else catches on and nobody goes). But there are always other ceremonies to take the place of those which are discontinued.

Afternoon in Hyde Park: waiting to see the Princess of Wales. ILN, *1889*

The London Season reached its zenith in the 1890s. By then, some of its manifestations were already on the decline, but the majority had reached their fullest glory and the overall pattern had become as crystallised as it would ever be. In earlier decades it was still growing and extending; during the Edwardian period it was starting to crumble and disintegrate. So as far as possible I have concentrated on the last decade of Victoria's reign, but I have not felt it necessary to be too dogmatic about this, for fluctuations in fashion were marginal compared with the overall persistence of the phenomenon as a whole.

I have called my book 'a social study' because it is as a social phenomenon that I believe the London Season to be worth examination. But I do not believe that my aim can be achieved by objective analysis alone, any more than the religious ceremonies of a savage tribe can be evaluated without a positive effort to enter into the participants' state of mind. So I have tried wherever possible to find others to express their opinions and even to detail the facts—people who were themselves involved, and whose individual response will help us to feel, as well as see, what it was like to be swept up in the London Season. I have tried—and I urge you to try—to be sympathetic. Much of what you read in these pages seems nauseating to our modern morality, even more seems unbelievably tedious, and the whole thing appears wasteful and unjust. But even if we end by condemning, let us start by trying to understand; and to understand, we must try to re-live the Season as it was lived by that strange race of 'genteel' folk whom Matthew Arnold dubbed 'Barbarians' but who considered themselves the élite of the social structure. Here in the London Season—the party that lasted for a hundred days and nights of almost unceasing activity—are our young barbarians at play.

Chapter 1
SOCIETY

The London Season was, in principle, open to all who cared to take part. Anyone could attend its more public manifestations—riding in Rotten Row, sitting or strolling in the fashionable areas of Hyde Park, patronising the favoured sporting events. If they could succeed in obtaining an invitation, anyone could attend the private functions too. But in practice the Season was a minority affair. Only a tiny fraction of the population took part—that fraction known, to themselves and to others, as 'Society'.

Who or what was 'Society'? The word in this context is ultimately undefinable, but this hasn't prevented a great many people trying to define it, and such an attempt is fundamental to our own inquiry because the London Season was the creation of Society, and owed its character to Society's tastes and values. If we are to understand the Season, we must first understand Society.

One of the many definitions put forward is purely quantitative—'the upper ten

Princess Alexandra, with her sister the future Czarina Maria Feodorovna. ILN, 1873

thousand'. Mathematically speaking, this means about one in 3000 of the population of late Victorian England. But what is meant by 'upper'? Clearly some kind of an élite is presupposed, and we shall indeed find that 'society' is to some degree interchangeable with 'aristocracy'—but only up to a point. An aristocracy implies rule by the best people, but nobody ever pretended that Society was made up of the best people by any conceivable definition of the word, even though 'the best people' was another of the paraphrases offered by the definers. At most, you could say of the aristocracy that it was composed of the descendants of people who at one or another period of history had proved themselves best at something or other—which could mean best at ruling or fighting battles but was equally likely to mean best at robbing, pimping or winning a royal mistress's favour.

By the mid-nineteenth century the aristocracy was no longer all that it had once been. The Reform Bill had deprived it of much of its political authority; the big names in politics were as likely to be the Gladstones and Disraelis as the Salisburys and Devonshires. The 1851 Great Exhibition had publicly demonstrated the contribution to Britain's greatness made by her manufacturers and working people. The face of Britain reflected changes which affected the aristocracy. Their big houses and wide estates made up much of the face of the land, but more and more they were neighboured by mines and mills, railways and canals. The towns had acquired a larger say in the affairs of the nation, the country relatively less: and even in the country, new landowners were increasing their stakes beside the old landed gentry.

All this is not to say that the aristocrats had lost their power: simply that now they had to share it with others. Despite the growth of industry, they still possessed the lion's share of the wealth of the country too. And with power and wealth went privilege: most people in England regarded a man or woman who happened to possess a title as someone innately superior. If the aristocracy continued to think of itself as an élite, most of their fellow-countrymen were happy enough to encourage them to think so. The Countess of Warwick, who, though she ended as a socialist, had as Lady Brooke been one of Society's 'stars' in the early 1890s, wrote of that period:

> When I came out, social prestige meant something. There was a definite aristocratic society of the landowning families. These families owned then practically the whole of the land of England. It was difficult to enter that society from the outside, and impossible unless Royalty approved. The Prince of Wales* was broadish-minded and inclined to welcome some of the professional class. A few doctors and artists were accepted. Sometimes a rich manufacturer might be able to poke his nose in, but he caught it for his temerity no matter how rich he might be. Political people were included, and any outstanding man or woman, say an explorer or a musician, but brains were rarely appreciated and literary people and intellectuals were not welcome. As for newspaper men, their entry was unheard of. Society did not want to be made to think.

*No hint here that she was at one time his mistress.

Society

Du Maurier, Punch, *1880*

WHERE THE SHOE PINCHES.

1880.

Eldest Daughter. "I think you might let me come out, Mamma! I'm twenty, you know, and surely I've finished my education!"

Festive Mamma (by no means prepared to act the part of Chaperone and Wallflower). "Not yet, my love. Society is so hollow! I really must preserve that sweet girlish freshness of yours a little while longer!"

Pillars of society: Edward VII as seen by Thony in Simplicissimus, 1900; Viscount Melgund, a noted sportsman of the 1890s; Frances Evelyn, Countess of Warwick, in 1889; and (below right) the incomparable Lily Langtry

So, though 'Society' and the aristocracy were not interchangeable terms, it was nevertheless to the aristocracy that Society looked for its leaders. Here is what the anonymous columnist of *The Ladies' Realm* wrote in 1896:

'Is there such a world?' the scoffer asks who has been surfeited with 'Society' novels (so-called) and fictitious 'Society' descriptions of the 'smart' set. I answer 'Yes' unhesitatingly. We have only to call to mind the names of the ladies who are the recognised leaders of Society. I don't mean the wives of the nouveaux riches, of the haute Juiverie, or of the Anglicised Americans who are always advertising themselves and their parties in the newspapers. These may entertain Society, amuse and feed it, but they will never *LEAD* it. That remains with those who have the right, and who care to exercise that right. Who are they? To answer this we have only to recall the names of the great ladies who have entertained considerably of late years, and whose houses are known as places where one meets all that is best in Society today . . . the following stand out pre-eminent as grandes dames to the finger-tips: the Duchess of Buccleugh, the Duchess of Devonshire, Lady Londonderry, Lady Cadogan, Lady Ilchester, and Lady Ellesmere . . . When we talk of Society we naturally look to them, and others like them, as its true representatives and leaders.

So Society was an élite, headed by the aristocracy, into which outsiders were permitted to break so long as they behaved themselves and offered something by way of inducement—money, or what money could buy; amusement; a talent for conversation; beauty. If you had any of these wares, you could hope to sell them in Society's market; and if you had them in abundance, you could hope for such rewards as came the way of the daughter of a priest from the Channel Islands, who married a shipowner named Langtry and took London by storm in the 1870s, winning her way—so the legend has it—with a single black dress (though possibly achieving even more without it). Many young ladies made it to the Prince of Wales's bed; few others had Society clambering on to chairs to get a better look at them.

In 1903 Pascoe—still in his disillusioned frame of mind—noted that Society was growing more flexible, less exclusive:

Society today is open to almost anyone who has a mind to enter it, if he has enough wealth, decent manners, sufficient 'push', if he races, yachts, sports, and entertains liberally, gets into Parliament, or makes himself of service politically, or buys a newspaper, or shows himself strong in 'the City', or does something or other first of all to make himself known.

Women find far more difficulty in entering the large-lettered London Society than men. Members of their own sex are the veriest dragons on watch and ward to keep them out. We cannot say we pity those ladies who do not succeed in getting beyond the outer gate. Society in the aggregate, big capital or small, is made up of the bores and the bored.

An American journalist, George W. Smalley, reported less cynically to *Harpers Magazine* in 1897:

I will venture to say of Society that it draws the best from all these departments of life, so far as they will consent to be drawn. This it does, not because it cares overmuch for rank or riches, for art or for literature, still less for science, but because it cares for excellence. It cares for a man who has pushed his way to the front; to have made his way to the front anywhere is *prima facie* evidence that he belongs to that company of the best, which only remains the best on condition of being continually recruited.

The system had its dangers. How were people to know the 'best' when they saw it? Might not a heavy bombardment of 'push' make a breach where 'bestness' with no force behind it would fail to make any impact? In short, wasn't Society in continual danger of being conned? Yes, thought Pascoe:

If you push down to the base of Society, you will find it rooted in pushfulness. A few persons of good birth and breeding, of congenial pursuits, tastes, or habits of good reading, let us say, or of a nice taste in art or music, or interested in some other subject,

Du Maurier,
Punch, *1874*

REFINEMENTS OF MODERN SPEECH.

Female Exquisite. " QUITE A NICE BALL AT MRS. MILLEFLEURS', WASN'T IT ?"
Male Ditto. " VERY QUITE. INDEED, REALLY MOST QUITE !"

meet occasionally at each other's house, to dine or for other friendly and pleasant inter-course. Then some less well-bred, interesting or entertaining personage in some way or other gains admission to the coterie. Someone suggests 'Why not invite him?' In a weak moment, the company good-naturedly yields. Then someone else seeks admission, and then someone else, and so it goes on—and by-and-by the original company is left with none of its old members, and the new set stand in their stead, and think of themselves as Society with a big capital letter.

Another correspondent to *Harpers Magazine*—anonymous this time—goes into greater detail regarding how to break into Society:

This status can be attained by any man whatever who possesses a suit of evening clothes and a fair amount of manners. Such a one will have no difficulty in getting an invitation to an ordinary dance in the less fashionable circles. Once there, he must get introduced to one or two of the matrons present who stand highest on the social ladder, and, if possible, have ugly daughters. He must dance, or pretend to dance, assiduously with the children, and take the mothers themselves to supper. If one of the latter gives a dance herself, or is asked for men's names by a friend, the aspirant will not be forgotten, and will get his name down on a list. He has then merely to continue this process as he rises in the world, with a proper devotion to leaving cards, calls, etc., and in a couple of years no ball or drum will be inaccessible to him.

With women it is different. Should they be neither fast, beautiful nor rich, they will find the steps of 'high life' hard to climb. Those who come under this description will have no difficulty. If they are in the first category, which in spite of certain morbid writers is still rare in England, they may get taken up by some nobleman or great personage, when they will become fashionable in a particular set, and be invited to the 'frisky matron' balls. But the august mothers of society will look coldly on them, and they will pine in vain for invitations to the old established houses.

Beauty, if accompanied by sobriety, can gain admission to any portal. The fair maiden having been first seen at a place of public entertainment, some enterprising woman, observing a chance of making her parties talked about, will send the stranger a card of invitation, mother and all. If she should be a success, no entertainment will be considered complete without her, and rich and great will tumble over each other in their civilities.

The method by which the rich climb the ladder can easily be described. In the first place, they must give a ball and secure the patronage of some lady within the charmed circle of the grande monde. She will probably be not very far within, perhaps the wife of a baronet or an Irish peer. This patroness sends out the invitations with her own compliments to all persons on her own list, and to many who are not on, but who she thinks will come. She extols, morning, noon, and night, the integrity of her protégés, and the splendours of the coming entertainment. She lets her female friends know that the decoration of the front landing will cost £700, her male acquaintance that £1000 will be spent on the supper. The first attempt will very likely be a partial failure. Few 'smart' people will appear; the guests will sneer at the host instead of dancing with the daughters. But they will see the front landing, eat the supper, and talk about both afterward. Consequently when in a short time a second ball is announced, there will be a rush for invitations; the donors will receive cards from all quarters themselves, and may be considered henceforth 'in society'.

The reference to fast women, incidentally, is almost certainly an allusion to the circle dominated by Edward, Prince of Wales, generally known as 'the Marlborough House set'. The Prince did more than anyone else to break down the barriers of the old formal society, openly differing from his mother's standards in this respect. His taste in women was for the 'fast and chaffy', and Lily Langtry may be regarded as typical. But not all Society followed where the Prince led; many of the great houses of Park Lane were harder to get into than Marlborough House—*particularly* if you were fast and chaffy.

Winning the entrée to Society was only the first step, though it was admittedly the biggest one. Once there, you had to be able to stay there. This was simply a matter of conforming; Society was like a club, and if you joined the club you tacitly accepted an obligation to observe its rules. As Smalley said:

> You must not only be in society, but of it. You must be of the brotherhood . . . There is a freemasonry to which you must belong. It is useless to enter the lodge as a spectator.

Society had its own rules of conduct, none the less rigorous for being unwritten. The Duke of Manchester, in his memoirs, tells of a young man who got drunk and behaved unbecomingly in the presence of ladies. In fact, as the Duke describes it, the young man's behaviour doesn't appear to have been notably outrageous when compared to what went on at some aristocratic gatherings of the period. Nonetheless, some of his fellows considered he had overstepped the mark; he was arraigned and formally tried, and sentence was passed that he should volunteer for the Boer War, then conveniently raging—and should not return. He went—and he did not return.

No doubt such an event was exceptional; but it gives us nevertheless a glimpse of the code of conduct which Society considered it had a duty to live by, and which bolstered up its own sense of being an élite. To justify their privileges, members of Society had to prove that they were 'better' than the unprivileged; and by subscribing to a code of conduct which they believed to be exclusive to 'gentlemen' as opposed to 'cads', they gave themselves the necessary injection of superiority.

For all that, their code was a realistic one, very conveniently adapted to their way of life. Here is the Countess of Warwick again:

> Nearly all the young men had mistresses, so most bridegrooms had a second establishment to pension off or maintain. The only thing that mattered was that there should be no scandal; everything was all right if only it was kept quiet, hushed up, covered. If a Society woman met a man—even her own brother—in the park or in a restaurant, when he was accompanied by his mistress or an actress, he would not raise his hat to her. He cut her, and she understood.
>
> In my circle there was a kind of freemasonry of conduct. We could be and do as we liked according to the code. The unforgivable sin was to give away any member of our group. That was class loyalty, I suppose, but we had no name for it.

Differing standards were imposed at different levels of Society. A contemporary observer noted, with reluctant admiration, in *The Cosmopolitan* (1902):

> The older families during the reign of Queen Victoria were entirely secure in their haughty position. They refused to recognise the actress-wife of a nobleman, however high her title. Not only did they refrain from inviting her to their own houses, but they were not likely to even lay eyes on her except perhaps at church or driving in Hyde Park, where a glance through lorgnettes poised haughtily was the only recognition she obtained.

But this was the extreme attitude, maintained only by those whose high position led them to identify with the views which Queen Victoria was known to hold. Such maintainers of the old moral standards—which incidentally were not all that old, being largely created in the course of the Victorian era—were gradually left higher and drier by the rest of Society, though respect for them increased proportionately. And of course, though membership of Society spanned all age groups, it was the younger members who participated most enthusiastically.

Various forces were acting at the same time to erode the old standards. Many of

Scandal and luxury: comments by Funny Folks ('A Mission to Mayfair': the unemployed discuss employing themselves in improving the moral condition of the idle upper classes), 1886, and Kind Words ('Ices: where are they more enjoyed?'), 1878

them can be summed up by saying that there was a general recognition that 'kind hearts are more than coronets'. The work of Darwin; the theology of Charles Kingsley; the moral philosophy of John Stuart Mill and Matthew Arnold; the political changes forced on the country by the radical MPs from Lancashire and other 'remote' districts—all these, though Society may have taken little direct notice of them, were influencing the country's climate of opinion, and indirectly affecting people's ideas about Society and ultimately Society's ideas about itself.

So when we speak of Society, we must not think of it as entirely homogeneous. To quote that perceptive American observer George Smalley once again:

'That girl seems to know you, George!' An awkward encounter in Regent Street. The Day's Doings, 1871

Society

If it be possible to generalise on such a matter, what is now called Society in London is made up of sets or separate coteries, each a society in itself, and all together combining into one very loosely organised whole. At the head of all these, from a purely fashionable point of view, is the Marlborough House set, meaning the Prince and Princess of Wales and their friends and associates. It is not necessary to speak of the Queen, because the Queen withdrew from Society on the death of the Prince Consort, and has never returned to it. Nor need the court, properly so classed, be considered. Drawing Rooms and Levees are held regularly, and it is still considered that a presentation at court is a certificate of social admissibility. The number of presentations is, however, very large, and is regulated upon principles very different from those which society adopts as tests or standards of admission to any of its many cliques. To be excluded from court would be, as a rule, a dis-qualification for the best or smartest society. Even to this rule there are brilliant exceptions. The Prince of Wales is a law unto himself . . .

I have tried to get Society to define itself, and if what emerges is a vague and fragmentary impression, that is because Society was itself a vague and fragmentary institution. In the end, perhaps, there has never been a more practical definition offered than that of Abraham Hayward, celebrated as the author of *The Art of Dining*, who said succinctly: 'Society consists of the people we know.' This definition has the virtue of underlining what is perhaps the most important characteristic of Society in general: its self-consciousness. It is possible that there were people in the innermost circles of Society who were so born and bred to the purple, so oblivious to outward forces, that it never crossed their minds to consider the possibility that they might ever be anything but 'in'. But for the majority, being in Society was something that had to be worked at; one's position, however unassail-able it might appear, had to be kept in good repair and periodically buttressed by some kind of public demonstration. One had to be seen doing the right thing in the right place with the right people—and wearing the right clothes.

And that was one of the reasons for the London Season.

A Young Lady's VISION of "THE LONDON SEASON"

George Cruikshank, The Table Book, 1845

Chapter 2
THE SEASON

Many explanations have been offered as to how the London Season came into being. Most of them are probably true, for the fact is that the Season served more than one purpose and answered several different needs. However, nearly all these needs and purposes stemmed from a single and most important fact, which is basic to so many of the features of the Season: *most of the people who formed Society—and particularly those who provided Society with its leaders—were fundamentally country people.* They might have houses in London, but their real family headquarters were in castles and manors throughout the shires of England, from which they took their names. There, for three-quarters of the year, they lived their normal lives—hunting, managing their estates, busying themselves with the affairs of the county, some living usefully, others not.

For various reasons they needed to visit the nation's capital from time to time. Courtiers needed to keep in touch with the Court; politicians needed to attend Parliament (which until well after 1900 sat for only six months of the year, from February to August). In days when travel was difficult, it was more convenient for the powers of the land to gather in summer than in winter, so the tradition had grown up over the centuries that the political affairs of the nation could be allowed to look after themselves during the winter months. Then, when fairer weather arrived, the monarch would summon his nobles and his advisers.

So that was part of it, but only the beginning. Perhaps more important from a social point of view was the pressure exerted by the womenfolk. The lives of women —even of aristocratic women—were none too eventful in the country; you could not choose your neighbours, you had to make the most of such limited amusements as were available. So when my lord prepared to travel to London to lend a hand with running the country, he found his wives and daughters clamouring to accompany him. Gradually a tradition built up by which the household as a whole moved to London for the summer months. Then, while the head of the family was engaged in running the country, his women could meet their friends, go shopping, exchange news, give and attend parties, and, perhaps most important of all, size up the husband market for their daughters.

It was made all the easier by the fact that they knew they were missing nothing

Style-setting Paris fashions for 1899: dressed for an afternoon visit (above left); dressed for an evening party (left); dressed for five o'clock tea (above). La Mode Illustrée

Above *Beauty's single London season is over and her chances at an end. 1885*

by leaving the country at this time. The hunting season was over, the shooting season had not yet begun; and for a great many of the country gentry, hunting and shooting were the major occupations of their lives. The tedious gap between them might as well be filled by a stay in London as by anything else.

Why London? Life of a sort, no doubt, went on elsewhere—in Dublin or Edinburgh. But just as London had no political or commercial rival, so it had no social competitor. For the members of Society, it had to be London or nothing. So, for a great many aristocratic families, there grew up a tradition of migrating to the capital at the end of April, to stay till the end of August. If they possessed a town house, naturally they stayed there; if they didn't, they rented a suitable house, fully furnished. The wealthiest families maintained two complete and separate establishments in town and country: the less well-to-do carried their plate and tableware and linen with them when they migrated. In either case they took the chief household servants with them, leaving only a skeleton staff to caretake in the home not in use.

The morning after the ball. Magazine of Art, *1889*

When they were in the country, the town house was completely shut up; the furniture was draped with sheets, the windows were shuttered. If for any reason a member of the family had to come up to London out of season, he or she would camp out in some back room, or even stay at a hotel, rather than go to the trouble and expense of opening up the main rooms of the house.

These town houses were generally not very homelike—but then they didn't have to be, for the activities which were transacted there during the Season were not those of normal home life. What was needed was space to entertain in, and rooms to eat and sleep in—and really that was all. Living—living in the normal sense—was something you did back in the country. You hadn't come all the way to London to sit at home.

What had you come for? Reduced to basic concepts, the objects of those who created the London Season were: firstly, to provide as many opportunities for social intercourse as possible; secondly, to make these gatherings as enjoyable and varied as possible; thirdly, to keep them as exclusive as possible.

To some extent, Society 'adopted' existing activities and events and made them peculiarly its own. A perfect example of this is Ascot Races. But it also created its own activities and patterns, like the weekly Church Parade in Hyde Park before lunch on Sunday. The programme was only loosely related to the calendar, as *Harpers Magazine* noted in 1886:

> Neither the beginning nor the end of the London Season is marked in the almanac, and of the more important facts exhibited during its continuance there is none which will supply a test. It is not especially the dancing season, the riding-in-the-Row season, the Parliamentary season, the drum season, the bazaar season, or the garden-party season, but the season of all combined. These things are not born with it and do not die with it, but may be said to flourish with it, in the sense that painters are said to flourish irrespective of the date of their births and deaths.

And so, between the end of April and the end of July, when London was growing too warm for comfort and its pleasures were beginning to pall, an elaborate programme of functions, some of them public and some of them private, was gradually built up to meet these needs. Inevitably, since every invitation was something of a status symbol, there was a social pressure to pack in as many functions as the days— and nights—could be stretched to contain. The Duke of Manchester recalled:

> When one came to London for the Season then, one came prepared for an orgy of parties, and ivory cards fell like snowflakes. One could count on being two or three deep every

Opposite *At the Royal Academy Show.* Graphic, *1871*

evening in balls, to say nothing of having a choice of dinner-parties beforehand, as well as lunch and even breakfast parties.

During the earlier years of Victoria's reign—the happy years before Albert's death—the Court had to some extent given Society a lead. Thus in May 1851, in the space of only eight days, the royal pair held two Drawing-Rooms, two State Concerts and a State Ball. Then Albert died, and his widow retired completely from the social scene, never to return except in old age, and then only to the most formal functions.

This was what brought about the biggest difference between the situation in England and that in the France of Louis XIV: in the latter, the King had been the focus of the whole elaborate set-up, in the former the Court had become a vacuum. The social lead was taken by leading aristocrats—duchesses and countesses who would normally have played a secondary role. In principle, they deferred to the invisible Queen; but in practice it was they who reigned over Society, and invitations to the 'top' houses were sought as eagerly, if not more so, as those to a royal Drawing-Room.

Not everyone could aspire to an invitation to a ball at Marlborough House or a reception at Devonshire House; but there was no lack of alternative functions—I was going to say 'pleasures', but as I shall show, this was not always the appropriate word. In the 1890s the programme of events for the Season comprised:

PRIVATE FUNCTIONS

Balls and dances
Breakfast parties, lunch parties, dinner parties
Afternoon receptions, tea parties, at-homes
Garden parties
Afternoon concerts, musical evenings
Evening receptions ('kettledrums' or 'drums' for short)
Court receptions and Drawing-Rooms
Theatre and opera visits (generally with a dinner party
    before and a supper party after)
Afternoon visits to such out-of-town clubs as Hurlingham

PUBLIC FUNCTIONS

Race meetings, particularly the Derby, Ascot and Goodwood
Henley Regatta
The Eton *v.* Harrow cricket match, and other activities
    at these two schools
The Royal Academy, particularly the private view,
    and to a lesser extent other galleries.

THE EMPIRE PROMENADE.

Demi-mondaines at the 'Empire' Promenade. Living London, *1902*

All this against a continuous accompaniment of riding and driving in the Park, paying calls and leaving cards, club life for the men, shopping, restaurant visits, visits to music halls and other nocturnal diversions also for the men. All these combined to make up the Season; and yet the Season was greater than the sum of its parts.

The cost was formidable. It was possible to take part in some of the Season's activities without having money to spend—it cost nothing to stroll in Hyde Park— but anyone who planned to participate at all fully had to be prepared to spend, spend and spend again. Even in an age when income tax was a shilling in the pound the expense would cripple all but the very well-heeled. A gentleman might be able to buy a tolerable suit for less than £10, but his wife and daughters would be unlikely to feel they could hold their own at Ascot in dresses costing less than £50 apiece—Lily Langtry's Paris dresses cost twice that amount, the equivalent of £500 and more today. If a lady made any pretence at keeping up with fashion, she would need many, many such dresses in the course of the Season. An article in the *Harms-*

worth London Magazine for October 1901 was entitled 'The Impossibility of Dressing on £1000 a year' and proved with utter seriousness that this was indeed the case for a woman with any pretensions to a place in fashionable—and fashion-conscious—Society.

Some items, admittedly, were not too dear. That essential commodity, domestic labour, was relatively cheap enough, with housemaids at around the £20-a-year mark and only the most senior servants drawing more than £1 a week. Yet the establishment of even a fairly modest, fashionable household would comprise a butler, two or three footmen, a chef or cook and probably a second, a couple of kitchen maids, two or three housemaids, a lady's maid for each adult lady in the family and a valet for each man, a page and/or boots, one or two coachmen and one or two grooms—which adds up to quite a substantial wages bill. And they all had to be housed and fed.

Probably the most costly item was entertaining—and entertaining was something you simply had to do if you expected to be asked out in your turn. Only the wittiest of men and the most beautiful of women could be held to have paid for their suppers with their bon mots and their good looks. To entertain meant to fork out the money for unlimited food and drink, for flowers and decorations, for music (generally a band), for waiters and other additional servants: not to mention new dresses for the hostess and her daughters.

And so it all added up: entertainment, accommodation, everyday food and drink for the whole household, clothes. Then there was transport—your own carriages or vehicles hired for the Season, the horses (which could also be hired) and their maintenance, and countless hansom cab journeys to speed you from one engagement to the next. And a profusion of incidentals—tickets for the theatre and the opera, the hire of a houseboat at Henley, subscription to clubs, and box after box of visiting cards, all helping the cost of the Season to mount up week by whirling week. The Season could never have survived as an institution had there not been many hundreds of people who, quite simply, never needed to take cost into account.

Chapter 3

THE MOST EXCLUSIVE VILLAGE IN THE WORLD

Geography played a vital part in making the Season what it was. We shan't begin to get the feel of London Society until we realise in how compact an area that life was lived. Except for a very few special events—the race meetings at Epsom, Ascot and Goodwood, the Regatta at Henley, and so forth—almost every event in the calendar occurred in London, in the West End, and in certain parts of the West End of London at that.

Naturally, not everyone could hope to live within the charmed circle; but the majority did, and the others clustered round as close as they could, like medieval villagers huddling round the walls of the castle that would protect them. The heart of Society beat in Mayfair, a haphazard maze of streets and squares to the north of Piccadilly, and round St James's Street, a smaller but no less maze-like district to the

Regent Street in the season. ILN, *1866*

Park Lane.
ILN, *1864*

south of the same street. Piccadilly itself was the High Street of the village, where each and every building had its part to play in the daily life of Society—housing shops, clubs, galleries, or simply friends and acquaintances.

Piccadilly Circus, at the east end of the street, was for most purposes the frontier of the smart area. Immediately beyond it was Theatreland, together with restaurants conveniently located for theatre parties to patronise. Here, too, were the haunts of vice which the gentlemen might patronise when the ladies had gone home to bed. Regent Street, which during the day attracted the smartest ladies to the shops and stores, by night offered their menfolk different attractions.

Men and women would find virtually all their shopping requirements met on their own doorstep—if not in Mayfair or the St James area, then in Regent Street, Oxford Street, the Haymarket. Only for special purchases did they need to venture farther afield—to Long Acre, perhaps, to inspect a new carriage, or to the Strand for a pair of field-glasses for the races.

The other fashionable residential area was Belgravia, to the west of Green Park, a spacious development of wide streets and handsome squares created by Thomas Cubitt earlier in the nineteenth century. Never quite so select as Mayfair or St James, it offered more recent arrivals on the social scene a chance to acquire a family house which could rival in size and splendour, if not in convenience of location, the great houses of Berkeley and Grosvenor Squares. Next down the scale came the ring of districts surrounding the charmed circle—Knightsbridge, Bayswater, Marylebone: all pleasant enough, but with only a back-of-the-stalls view of the events on the fashionable stage.

So a family would, if possible, hope to own or rent a house in Mayfair; a single man would find lodgings suited to his means in St James or Mayfair; more transient visitors would put up at one of the many grand hotels in the area. The family houses were in big streets or squares which had little mews streets running behind, where the carriages were kept. The streets themselves were busy throughout the day with carriages and cabs, conveying the inhabitants of the village from one end of it to the other.

The role of Lord of the Manor of Society's village was shared by Victoria and her son Albert Edward. Both of them lived close to the Village—Victoria at Buckingham

Below and opposite Bird's-eye views of the West End. G. W. Ruffle, 1900

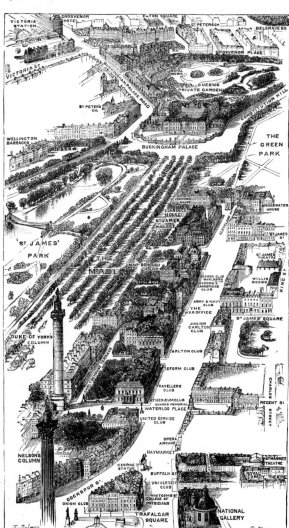

FROM CHARING CROSS, THROUGH PALL MALL, TO PIMLICO

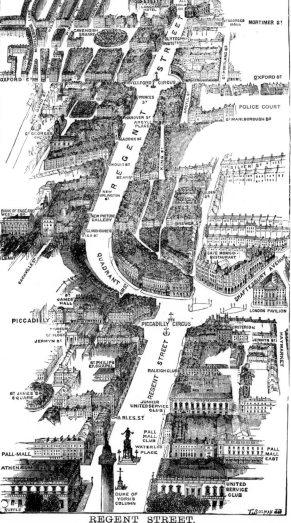

REGENT STREET,
FROM WATERLOO PLACE TO PORTLAND PLACE.

Palace, adjacent to St James's Park and separating Belgravia from St James; and the Prince at Marlborough House, in St James. Each establishment had its part to play in the events of the Season, though only the Prince and Princess participated in the daily round of the Season.

Every village should ideally have its village green; Society had a choice of parks to play in, but there was never any doubt what a gentleman or lady meant when they referred to 'the' park—it was always Hyde Park. Green Park and St James's Park might be handy for occasional strolls, or as a short cut from A to B; but only Hyde Park was privileged to be the scene of Society's fashionable gatherings and get-togethers. The very best houses of all were situated on Park Lane, the westernmost edge of Mayfair which looks out over the Park.

And so everyone who was anyone in Society lived within a few minutes' distance from everyone else. If necessary, you could walk to anyone's house, though usually you were in too much of a hurry. The Park, the shops, the clubs, all were in easy reach, and to reach them you walked down streets which housed other clubs and

→ 34

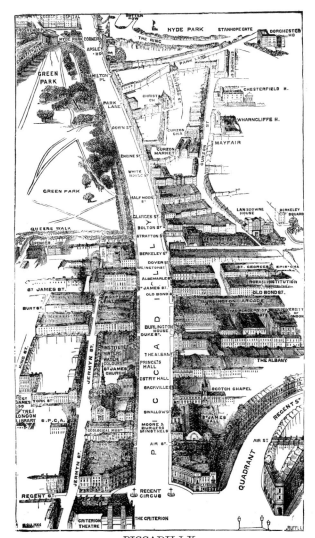

PICCADILLY,
FROM THE HAYMARKET TO HYDE PARK CORNER.

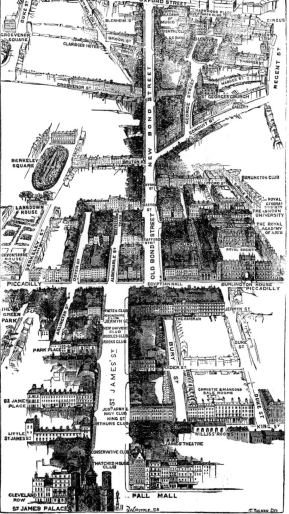

ST. JAMES'S STREET, AND OLD AND NEW BOND STREETS.

Belgravia out of doors. Richard Doyle, Cornhill Magazine, c. 1850

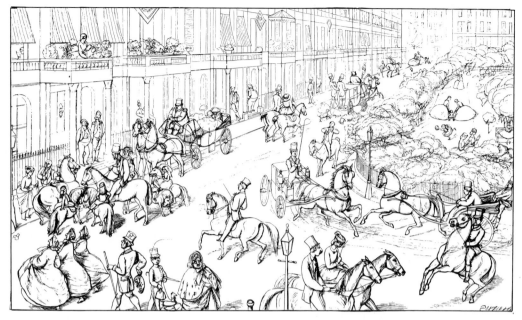

Below Belgrave Square. Cassell's Old and New London, c. 1875

The Most Exclusive Village In The World

Piccadilly.
Century, 1888

Below The
Prince of Wales
drives out of
Marlborough
House. London
of today, *1890*

shops patronised by your friends and acquaintances, or passed your friends' and acquaintances' homes. Their carriages overtook you as you walked, or you caught a glimpse of them hurrying by in a cab. If Lady A invited you to lunch, chances were that you would only have to travel a hundred yards to get to her house; a dance might be next door; even the theatre and the opera were only a mile or so away, hardly more than the length of the drive back home in the country. The pavements were busy with people, many of whom could be friends and acquaintances; a man in the social swim would be unfortunate if he walked down Piccadilly without running into someone he knew.

In short, it was a village life; better, it was a very exclusive village life, because everyone you knew or cared to know had come to live in the same village. For folk who spent the greater part of the year scattered across the counties of England it was a welcome change; for three hectic months they had the chance to see as much of one another as they wanted—and they made the most of that chance.

Chapter 4
THE DAILY ROUND

Whatever else the life of a society lady may be, it is not one of idleness. No one can attain to a high social position without finding innumerable responsibilities, ties and occupations to fill the day. A woman of fashion may be self-indulgent, but can scarcely be lazy, for even the pleasures of life are so strenuous and so fatiguing that she is drawn in spite of herself into the vortex of energy. Play has become nearly as laborious as actual work.

So wrote Lady Violet Greville in an article entitled 'Round the Clock with a Society Woman' in the *London Magazine* for 1904. The daily round of the Season, once it had been programmed, demanded a great deal from its adherents. Many flagged after a while, many more uttered complaints, yet the pace never slackened. Though it would certainly be going too far to say that there was never a dull moment, for those who took their participation seriously every moment of the day and half the night was taken up with doing *something*. The following account is of a Society lady's day, continued from the extract quoted above and written by a lady who seems to have taken upon herself the task of describing the ways of the best people for the edification of the second-best—perhaps in a spirit of missionary zeal, perhaps because she needed the pin-money. At any rate, her name crops up in one contemporary periodical after another telling those outside Society what life was like on the inside:

The society lady is an early riser; the multiplicity of her occupations does not allow her to lie in bed. She is on her horse in the Park unceremoniously dressed in a straw hat, a loose coat, white shirt and thin short habit by 9 a.m. on a summer's morning, after a breakfast consisting only of a cup of tea and a slice of bread and butter. A brisk canter, a few turns up and down the Row, a chat with friends, and, her nerves refreshed and strengthened, she is back home again at 10 a.m., ready for the day's work. She has her large correspondence to get through, innumerable notes to answer, telegrams to send, her children to see, arrangements to make, dinner and luncheon to order . . . Wrapped in a light muslin négligée, she transacts her business in her own private boudoir, glued often to the telephone which now constitutes the necessary equipment of every well-appointed house; she dictates to her secretary and typewriter,* reads the leading articles in the paper, or wields the pen herself with the readiness and energy of the practised scribe.

---

*The word was then used both for the machine and for its user.

The Daily Round

Opposite
Her morning ride. Cassells
1892

Perhaps some important shopping or an appointment with the dressmaker, on no account to be missed, claims her attention, in which case she quickly slips on a simple morning dress of linen or piqué, and a plain straw hat with a bunch of roses, and drives out about twelve o'clock with a friend, bent on the same mission, who has come to fetch her. She returns a little before two o'clock to change into a smart afternoon gown, and attend a luncheon party or receive her own guests at this elaborate meal. The table is decked with flowers, and several courses follow in succession, from fish or daintily prepared eggs, to an entrée, a roast, cold ham, pie or beef on the side table, and a sweet, fruit, coffee, liqueurs and cigarettes. The latter are now always offered to ladies, many of whom smoke habitually. The company rarely separate before four o'clock, and often comprise a heterogeneous assortment of pretty women, ambitious politicians, popular actors, famous soldiers, literary men and millionaires.

Now perhaps the society lady may snatch a few minutes to read a book or cut the pages of the newest novel, about which she is expected to talk at dinner; but unless contrary orders have been given, the door opens frequently, and admits a constant stream of visitors, some of whom stay to tea, which is daintily served on little tables covered by lace-trimmed table-cloths, with a profusion of pretty silver and rare china. Each lady has her own speciality for tea, some kind of savoury sandwich or appetising cake, for a hostess takes pride in her tea-table.

By this time the carriage is at the door for the afternoon drive and the smart pair of horses in the C-spring Victoria are champing their bits outside to the admiration of the passer-by. After half an hour of card-leaving, it is easy to flit down to Richmond or Coombe.

The dinner hour in London grows later and later, few people sit down now before half-past eight or nine o'clock, which indeed seems early enough when one considers that after dinner comes a rubber of bridge, or an evening party and concert, followed by a ball which lasts perhaps till daylight. Truly, a society woman may well feel tired at the end of so busy a day . . .

Judging by the tone of voice of the whole piece, there is no irony intended in that concluding sentence. The theme of 'hard work' is also taken up in a complementary masculine excerpt, in which the journalist Douglas Jerrold speaks of doing London during the Season with his collaborator, the French artist Gustave Doré, whom he designates as his fellow-pilgrim. The following account comes from their book, *London: A Pilgrimage*, which appeared in 1872:

Indeed, a good, a thorough day in the Season means hard work. The early canter, when the pale emerald glories of the spring foliage and the misty blue of the sky make a cool, invigorating morning, disposes the weariest for breakfast, the morning papers, and the inevitable pile of letters.

How shall we spend the morning? My fellow Pilgrim declares for the Park again; for a lazy cigar, and a study of Fashion riding or walking hard, in the bracing air, to get over the fatigues of yesterday.

The high-bred, delicate, rose-tinted beauty of women and children; the courage and comeliness of the amazons—the calm, solid air of their cavaliers; the perfect horses; the severe simplicity and perfect appointments of the liveried attendants; the genial air of quiet strength and grace which is upon all the scene—are strange to the mind of the habitué of the Bois de Boulogne. He returns to the Park again and again, and will have his afternoon turn along the Ladies' Mile, let his engagements be what they may.

'Let us have an hour in the Royal Academy before lunch; we shall see some types of true British beauty,' is the second suggestion of the day. Here, in their morning freshness, we find troops of the partners of last evening. Perhaps they look their best in their early toilettes and with their homelier expression.

Lunch, a little laziness, and a little letter-writing, bring us to the hour for calls; to a fancy bazaar; to a garden party; to a talk and tea in the charming grounds of Lambeth Palace, or to a dancing, flirting or argumentative tea!

And the day is far away still from its close!

We are at the point of the great solemnity of the day—dinner . . . It has been observed that the worst of a dinner-table is that you must leave it. And you must leave it early, and be very discreet at it, if you would be welcome first at the soirée of the learned Society; then at the Deanery; then at the Opera; and lastly as you look in at a ball or two, before you go home in the palest hour of the morning, when the sweep—the early London riser—is the only creature at work.

Comparison with other accounts confirms that these were indeed representative days in the Season. But the regime permitted a reasonable choice of options, either to suit individual tastes and ages or to meet particular circumstances. To start with,

Coaching to Hurlingham.
Graphic, *1895*

The Daily Round

Above *The society woman deals with her correspondence in her boudoir, and visits the nursery.* London Magazine, *1904*

Right *At the milliner's.* Graphic, *1895*

not everybody wanted to get up quite so early. If you had been dancing till dawn, the thought of riding in the Park at 9 a.m. might not seem so attractive—even the most enthusiastic débutante (a word first used in 1837 to describe a girl coming out into society) might need a longer rest to prepare her for the rigours of the day. Besides, it often rains in England: the Park swept with a drenching downpour is a very different place from the Park shimmering with early morning haze at the start of a dazzling summer's day.

Another morning option was the breakfast party, favoured more by men than by women. It gave politicians and men of affairs a chance to talk together informally but without the distractions which accompanied most of Society's gatherings. It was also an agreeable way of starting the day with something substantial if an excursion into the country was planned which would prevent any kind of lunch party. Breakfast parties, as we shall see, were fairly elaborate affairs and nobody who had attended one would be likely to feel in the mood for lunch.

The interval between breakfast and lunch, which Lady Greville's fashionable lady spent shopping, could be spent in other ways if you had already exceeded your dress allowance for the month. The two hours before lunch were favoured by riders in the Park, and for ladies who enjoyed driving their own carriages. This was an animated time of day in the Park, less formal than the afternoon session.

But it was the afternoon which offered the widest choice of amusements. A lady might stay at home and receive friends, or she could drive out to pay calls on others,

A charity bazaar. Graphic, *1895*

The Daily Round

Above *The Ladies' Kennel Club*. London Magazine, *1904*

Right *A fashionable flower show*. Graphic, *1872*

leaving cards and paying a series of courtesy calls—she could fit in half a dozen of
these with careful planning. Or she might attend a more formal function—an
afternoon concert, a private view at an art gallery, a garden party, a flower show,
some sporting event; or she could pay a visit to one of the clubs on the outskirts of
London, such as Hurlingham, Ranelagh or the Orleans. Here, there were such
diversions as pigeon shooting, croquet, lawn tennis or archery, in which she might
take part or simply be a spectator. A gentleman might play polo, a favourite spectator
sport for the ladies.

Another popular afternoon function was the charity bazaar, a somewhat hypo-
critical but generally harmless occupation which, to paraphrase Oscar Wilde, one
might describe as homage paid by wealth to poverty. An anonymous correspondent
writes in *Harpers Magazine* in 1886:

> Bazaars in London have developed amazingly of late years. There is no doubt that they
> present considerable attractions to 'frisky matrons' and to young ladies who have any
> themselves. Fashionable beauties play the part of shop-women, conceiving that they are
> laying up treasures in heaven, when in reality they are showing themselves to fresh
> audiences, and seeking excitement in a licence of manners that is not possible on other
> occasions. As the virtuous object of the bazaar elevates it above the laws of supply and

demand, its success depends chiefly upon the personal efforts of these saleswomen, who have to tease and wheedle visitors into buying. Anything, therefore, unusual, conspicuous or violent in the appearance or manners of a person who keeps a stall tends to attract buyers, the result being an increasing extravagance of dress and demeanour at these exhibitions.

For similar reasons it has been the custom of late years to give bazaars a particular cast, supported by scenery and fancy dress. Thus you have the 'Mediaeval Market' where ladies in peaked caps and turned-up shoes display modern manners and wares in mediaevally shaped stalls. Or the Shakespearean Bazaar, where Portia sells pincushions and Cleopatra buttonholes . . . Fascinating beauties force cups of tea down the throats of passers-by. Still more adventurous members of the same class tell fortunes and disagreeable truths in the guise of wizards, or play the banjo and send round the hat.

And then of course there were the special occasions, the highlights of the Season —Ascot, the Derby, Henley, Goodwood and so forth, all of which we shall be examining more closely later on. Keen race-goers easily found other meetings to attend, just as lovers of cricket could go to Lord's or the Kennington Oval, art-lovers could attend artistic shows and soirées, and so forth. But Lady Greville is fundamentally correct in suggesting that paying calls and leaving cards were the basic activities of the afternoon, and it will be worth examining these two activities in a little more detail for the light they throw on the way Society behaved.

LEAVING CARDS

A stock of visiting cards was an essential item in everyone's personal equipment. They were called for continuously throughout the day as identification to tradespeople and servants; but between equals they played an even more vital role in the elaborate game of etiquette. The following notes, culled from a variety of handbooks with titles such as *Manners and Rules of Good Society, or Solecisms to be Avoided* (by 'A Member of the Aristocracy'), show just how careful one had to be, for, as this author points out:

> The etiquette of card-leaving is a privilege which society places in the hands of ladies to govern and determine their acquaintanceships and intimacies, to regulate and decide whom they will, and whom they will not visit, whom they will admit to their friendship, and whom they will keep on the most distant footing, whose acquaintance they wish further to cultivate and whose to discontinue.

The practice of leaving cards principally devolved on the lady; a wife should leave cards for her husband as well as for herself. A young lady would not usually have a card of her own, but her name would be included with that of her mother— or other chaperon—if she was 'out'. If for any reason she was visiting without her mother, she would use her mother's card but draw a pencil through her mother's name.

The object of leaving cards was to signify that a call had been made; it was a gesture of politeness, and expected to be returned with equivalent politeness. A lady arriving in Town would immediately leave cards on all her acquaintances to tell them that she had arrived. The same happened when she left, in which case she would write 'PPC' (= *pour prendre congé*, to take leave) in the lower corner.

The actual leaving of the card went like this: the lady, waiting outside in her carriage, would ask her manservant to inquire if the lady of the house at which she was calling was 'at home'. If the answer was 'not at home' she would get him to hand in three cards—one of her own and two of her husband's. Her own card was for the mistress of the house, her husband's cards for both master and mistress. If the mistress of the house was 'at home', the visitor would, after making the call, leave two of her husband's cards on the hall table on leaving. She would not put them into the card-basket, or leave them on the drawing-room table, or offer them to her hostess; but she might on reaching the hall hand them silently to the manservant of the house, or she might wait till she got outside to her carriage again and then send them in by her own manservant. If other ladies of the family besides the hostess were included in the call, the visitor would turn down one corner.

Cards were left by every guest after invitations to the following entertainments: balls and dances, receptions, private theatricals, afternoon concerts, dinner parties. What is more, cards were left *even if the invitation had been refused*. They should be left the day after the entertainment, if possible, and certainly within the week. On these occasions the cards were left without inquiry as to whether the hostess was at home, except in the case of a dinner-party, which implied a greater degree of intimacy than the other entertainments listed.

A lady should not leave cards on another lady to whom she had but recently been introduced at a dinner-party or afternoon tea. She must first meet her several times in society and feel sure that her acquaintance is desirable, before venturing to leave her card. This was very delicate ground for the social climber; many must have been the agonising decisions debated and made before taking—or not taking—such a fateful step!

Leaving a card on someone left the ball in their court; it had to be 'returned'— that is to say, the recipient had to respond with a card-leaving of her own, within a week or ten days after receiving. A call must not be returned by a card only, or a card by a call. But a lady of higher rank could return a card by a call, which signified gracious condescension; or, less graciously, she could return a call by a card only. This would signify to the unhappy recipient that the senior lady wished the acquaintance to be of the slightest. If she did not wish there to be any continuance of the acquaintance at all, she would of course simply return neither card nor call— which would constitute an outright snub.

If a friend was ill, one left a card with the words 'to inquire after Lady So-and-So' written above the printed name. In return, a card was sent, probably by a servant, with the words 'return thanks for kind inquiries' written on it.

Card-leaving was not regarded as nearly so important for men. It was recognised that they had little time for this activity, and were not usually expected to conform as strictly as their womenfolk. But they were looked on with favour if they did. A bachelor was expected (and it was generally in his interest) to leave cards on the master and mistress of a house with which he was acquainted as soon as he was aware that they had arrived in Town. If he himself had been away, he would leave a card immediately after his return. He would leave one for the mistress of the house and one for its master. Even if his real interest in the house was neither the master nor the mistress but their pretty daughter, he would not leave a card for her but for her parents or chaperon. A gentleman did not leave his card upon a married lady, or the mistress of a house, however gracious or agreeable she had been to him, unless she expressly asked him to call or gave him to understand in an unmistakable manner that his doing so would be agreeable to her.

PAYING CALLS

Ladies stand upon strict and ceremonious etiquette with each other as regards both paying and receiving calls. When a call has not been made within a reasonable time, a coldness is apt to arise between ladies but slightly acquainted with each other. Some ladies take this omission good-naturedly or indifferently, while with others the acquaintance merges into a mere bowing acquaintance, to be subsequently dropped altogether.

(*Manners and Rules of Good Society*)

Paying calls was a kind of higher form of leaving cards. A similar protocol existed, dictating fairly rigidly on what occasions you paid calls, at what time of day, on whom you called, and how long you stayed.

A lady or gentleman might call on anyone with whom they were acquainted and to whom they had reason to suppose that the call would be agreeable. It did not imply any great degree of intimacy, but it was distinctly one up on simple card-leaving. Calling was of course an important stepping-stone in the process of social climbing, but a badly judged call could do irreparable damage.

A call was known as a 'morning' call even though it might be made in the afternoon or evening—the word 'morning' simply signified before dinner. One only paid calls literally in the morning—that is, before 1 p.m.—on intimate friends, in which case the rigid formality attached to call-paying didn't apply.

A rough-and-ready rule was that calls paid between 3 and 4 p.m. were ceremonious; those between 4 and 5 p.m. semi-ceremonious; those between 5 and 6 p.m. wholly friendly and without ceremony. The afternoon's call-paying was therefore a case of attending to business first, taking one's pleasure afterwards.

If the visit was simply a formal call, the hostess should not offer her visitor any refreshments; a call was *not* the equivalent of a tea-party. *A quarter of an hour was the absolute maximum duration for a ceremonious call.* When another visitor arrived, the first visitor would take her leave as soon as she conveniently could.

A gentleman when calling would take his hat and stick with him into the drawing room and hold them until he had shaken hands with his hostess. He would then either place them on a chair or table, or hold them in his hand. (If he was invited to

An aristo-cratic 'at home'. Cassells, c. *1890*

afternoon tea, however, he could leave his hat in the hall, with the implication that he was at home there.)

Card-leaving and call-paying give us a glimpse of the more punctilious side of Society life. Though not as fraught with rules as the Japanese tea-ceremony, they were nevertheless important rituals whose strict observance was considered to be an essential part of a member of Society's behaviour. Whatever one might do in private, Society insisted on a certain standard of public behaviour; to an outsider, such ceremonies might look like hypocrisy, but to Society people they were a kind

The Athenaeum *Club: the morning room.* ILN, *1893*

The Athenaeum Club, Pall Mall. ILN, *1893*

of safeguard against intrusion by people who 'did not know how to behave'.

As indicated above, these rituals were primarily the responsibility of the ladies. Men were encouraged to pay afternoon calls, but were not generally very responsive to such encouragement. For those not engaged in sporting activities, the favourite pastime was to retreat into one or other of the clubs—peaceful sanctuaries where women seldom if ever penetrated. A contemporary author, Robert Machray, notes in his book *The Night Side of London* (1902):

> The club-man of seventy or eighty years ago, who spent most of his evenings in his club gaming, drinking, gossiping, were he to come to life again and revisit his former haunt at his accustomed time o' night, would more probably than not find it almost empty. And were he to be told that clubs are most populous at the hour sacred to afternoon tea, he would not believe it, or if he did, he would get himself back in disgust to the shades again.

Machray counted about 125 respectable gentlemen's clubs in 1902 as against only 12 for ladies—a discrepancy on which he forbears to comment, but which was due quite simply to the fact that the Society lady had her own drawing-room to use for social purposes and needed no other: ladies' clubs were for those who had no drawing-room, and a lady who had no drawing-room had no place in Society. He adds: 'An ingenious American, fond of the statistical side of life, has calculated that the "recognised" London clubs have a membership of upwards of 100,000.' Most men in Society would have more than one club; a few 'collected' them, giving themselves a choice of places to go to according to their mood or even depending on which was nearest at hand at any given moment. Each club had its own distinctive character, in each he would meet a different set of people, each more or less congenial in its own way.

It is perhaps worth noting the better-known clubs and their distinctive characters, for by a man's clubs it was possible, if not to know him, at least provisionally to pigeonhole him.

The first and most important category comprised the political clubs. On the Tory side there was, first and foremost, the Carlton—the great party stronghold and a focus of activity on election nights and other critical occasions; others included the Junior Carlton, the Conservative, the Constitutional, the Junior Constitutional, and the Saint Stephen's—all names which had a good, solid ring to them. The Liberals had a more restricted choice: their headquarters was the Reform, noted for its cuisine, and others were the Devonshire, the Eighty, the National Liberal and the New Reform. Some of these were distinctly aristocratic, others more middle-class. There was, needless to say, considerable status attached to membership of the most exclusive of them.

'The bay window of our club'. London Society, *1864*

Another big group comprised the service clubs—the United Service (known to admirers as the 'Senior', to less reverent men as 'The Cripples' Home'), the Army and Navy (known as the 'Rag'), the Naval and Military, the East India United Service, the Junior Army and Navy, the Junior Naval and Military, the Cavalry and the Guards.

Sportsmen had a wide choice of clubs from the Alpine to the Victoria, some respectable, others distinctly raffish. The Turf was the most respectable and the most exclusive; the National Sporting Club one of the most 'professional'. The Travellers' Club, for which the qualification was simply to have travelled the equivalent of at least 500 miles in a straight line from London, was another well-known institution which may perhaps be categorised as 'sporting'.

Of social clubs which had gradually acquired a distinctive cast, some of the best known were the St James, favoured by diplomats; the Savile, the Authors', the Arundel and the Savage, patronised by practitioners or lovers of literature; the Arts, the Burlington and the Savage (again), favoured by artists and their patrons; the Garrick, the Green Room, the O.P. (Old Playgoers), used by actors and patrons of the drama.

Finally there were clubs which had no distinctive character, but which had their own more or less exclusive set of members. Arthur's, Boodle's, the New Lyric and the Athenaeum were especially noteworthy establishments, and of course there was the Marlborough in Pall Mall of which the Prince of Wales was a member.

In a sense, these gentlemen's clubs did not form part of the Season at all—if anything, they were a retreat from it, or from certain manifestations of it. But for many country gentlemen the clubs were used only during the Season, or in the course of occasional out-of-season visits to Town on business. Here they could meet their fellow-men away from the distracting influence of the ladies, and promote the affairs of the nation—or their own—informally and in comfort.

There were those, however, who felt the need for something more, social clubs where both men and women could meet in respectable surroundings but without incurring any debt of hospitality—a sort of neutral territory, in fact. In 1886 *Harpers* reported the advent of institutions designed to meet this need:

> In London, what may be called café and casino clubs have been established. At the former, such as the Bachelors' Club, ladies are invited to dine or sup by the members before or after the theatre.
>
> At the New Club, which is at present the only specimen of the latter class, a band plays every night at eleven, when persons who have been to the play, or have nothing in particular to do, drop in and drink coffee and smoke. There are weekly balls in the Season. Young ladies go to the balls, but the visitors on ordinary nights are mostly fashionable 'friskies'.

But these early foreshadowings of the twentieth-century night-club did not flourish: perhaps because there was still so much private entertaining that the need

The Daily Round

was not yet urgent enough, perhaps too because the growth of the restaurant business provided sufficient late-evening entertainment to satisfy most people. However, restaurants had by law to close on Saturday at midnight, so as not to intrude upon the Lord's Day: so for this one night of the week a club was formed at the end of the century, the Grafton, where people could go after the theatre for dancing and refreshment. The fact that it was described as 'favoured by actresses' suggests that the Grafton was only on the outer edge of respectability.

Most of the more popular kinds of diversion and activity which made up the daily round of the Season have now been mentioned, and we can sketch out in a rough-and-ready fashion the day's timetable, into which the various activities we shall be looking at more closely in later chapters had, somehow, to be fitted:

8 a.m.	Get up, if planning to go riding. Light breakfast.
9 a.m.	Ride in Park; or, if not riding, get up.
10 a.m.	Return from ride. Breakfast. Correspondence, business, planning of day's activities, future engagements etc.
11 a.m.	Breakfast party. Shopping. Instructions to servants etc.
12 a.m.	Riding or driving in the Park. Shopping. Calls on intimate friends. Visits to art galleries and exhibitions.
2 p.m.	Lunch.
3.30 p.m.	Afternoon concert. Outing to Hurlingham, Richmond etc. Formal calls.
4 p.m.	Garden party. Tea party at home. Charity bazaar. Afternoon calls. Men at club.
5 p.m.	Drive, ride or stroll in Park. Informal calls.
7 p.m.	Dinner if going to theatre.
8 p.m.	Dinner-party. Theatre or opera.
10 p.m.	Receptions, soirées.
11 p.m.	Balls, dances.
11.30 p.m.	Supper after theatre or opera.
1 a.m.	Supper at balls and dances.
3 a.m.	Balls usually end.

SUNDAY

Sunday was an awkward day for Society. However welcome it might be for those whose station in life required them to work in a factory or down a mine, it could hardly be said to be so essential to those whom a thoughtful providence had absolved from such necessities. However, as we have already seen, Society worked hard at its play, and a break in the social whirl was welcome in its own way to all but the most indefatigable dancers and party-goers. So there were no balls or dances on Sunday, and no formal calling.

But life had to go on, including social life. Not for Society, so clearly favoured by Heaven as it was, to spend the traditional Victorian Sunday of church services interspersed with bible-reading and meditation on texts. Due acknowledgment should be made, no doubt, to the Creator who had ordained that some should receive more of the things of this earth than others, and so many—if not most—of Society attended divine service on Sunday mornings. Needless to say, some churches were more fashionable than others, and you attended the one most congenial to your social status as well as your spiritual stance.

But morning service over, Society had done its duty by God for the week. The question now was, what to do after Church?

Early in the year 1888 the bench of Bishops in Convocation were much exercised about the way the upper and fashionable classes of London society observed the Sabbath. The Bishop of Exeter reminded his colleagues that there had lately been a very marked increase in the employment of the afternoon and evening of the

Hyde Park, church parade. La vie de Londres, 1890

Lord's Day by amusements of various kinds, which were duly reported in the newspapers of the following day. He gave examples:

> Those of recent date include formal dinner-parties, smoking concerts, theatrical and semi-theatrical performances, comic recitations, and amusing programmes of fun and frolic, exhibitions of jugglery, Sunday parades in Hyde Park, coach drives of clubs, the drags assembling at Hampton Court, Richmond, and other places of resort; the 'Sunday up the river'; boxing at the Pelican Club, lawn tennis, dances at clubs and private houses, exhibitions of the Wild West Show; Show Sunday in the studios of artists.

Some of these, the Bishop explained, were novelties in the way of profanation of the Lord's Day. The long lists of those present included eminent people in all walks of life. Their presence, he declared, 'testifies to very loose Sunday habits on the part of the rich and great and noble of the land. Such abuses of the Lord's Day evidence an insatiable desire for distraction and dissipation, a very low regard for the claims of the Word of God, and a determination to put away the restraints of religion.'

The worthy Bishop was undoubtedly right. Society as a whole did not intend to be restricted by religion, and the amount of lip-service it was prepared to pay was strictly limited. So, after Church was over and God had been duly thanked, as courtesy demanded from one gentleman to another, for doing his bit for another week, Society crossed over into the Park and, prayer-book in hand, congregated to plan the day's amusements and those of the week ahead.

Chapter 5
THE PARK

The significance of Hyde Park in the scheme of things can hardly be exaggerated. Here the once-a-year villagers gathered on their village green, neutral ground where they could give one another the once-over, meet casually without incurring any debt of hospitality, make public parade of likes or dislikes. Very little of real importance actually happened here, but a great deal was planned—and a great deal was subsequently post-mortemed.

Hyde Park had been the favourite rendezvous of the upper classes since the day King James I had thrown it open to the public. The surrounding districts had been almost rural then; as they were gradually covered over with houses and streets, the

Du Maurier,
Punch, *1887*

THE DEAD SEASON.   1887.

(*Showing how to be " In it " is to be " Out of it."*)

Snobbington. "Town seems more deserted than ever, *don't it*, Miss Masham?"
Miss Masham. "Quite. I've been up to the Top and back again Five times—there's positively *not a Soul in the Row!*"

Above
*'Costume
d'amazone'.*
La Mode
Illustrée, *1899*
Below *'The
English take
their pleasures
sadly'. Du
Maurier,*
Harpers
Monthly, *1885*

more vital Hyde Park became as a natural clearing, a breathing space. Once again it is important to remember that Society was made up of people whose roots were in the country: though they might be ready to exchange their rolling estates for narrow streets for a few weeks, fresh air and grass and trees were still their natural environment, and they probably felt more at home on the lawns of the Park than on the pavements of Regent Street and Piccadilly.

Nevertheless, it was not the rural character of the Park which most attracted Society. In the main they did not make use of more than a few restricted sections of it—the Rotten Row for riding, the Drive for driving, and the immediate hinterland of those two ways for sitting, strolling, chatting, flirting, eyeing and being eyed.

The Countess of Warwick expressively captures the atmosphere of the Park in the Season:

In the eighties and nineties there was only *one* Park, called Hyde; when we spoke of 'The Park' it was always Hyde Park near the Corner. If you entered by the Albert Memorial or Marble Arch you were certain to be making for that select spot lying between Albert and Grosvenor Gates. Here the small circle of Society with the big 'S' was sure of meeting all its members on morning ride or drive, or in the late afternoon between tea and dinner, in what was practically a daily Society Garden Party! Sometimes, engaged couples or the partners of illicit assignations wandered as far as the Serpentine banks, but there they were liable to meet 'Bayswater' and 'the people who rowed on the water', and all soon shuddered

back to the inviolate spot. In the late nineties 'Bayswater'—no other suburb was known—invaded the Society Church Parade on a Sunday morning, but these interlopers had scant welcome, and the little Society ranks closed up only the more exclusively by the Achilles statue.

My memory flew back to the noon daily drive of my phaeton with high-stepping chestnuts, or browns, or bays, eagerly recognised by admiring friends who crowded round on horseback or on foot when one pulled up at the entrance to the Row and chatted of the social round—of future meetings, of dances, lunches, and dinners within 'the Circle'. My horses were so well-known that they always made a stir. One 'booked' friends for luncheon, and perhaps drove them down Piccadilly prancing on the wide sweep of pavement, glancing up at the Turf Club window as a possible place to find an extra man for a dinner-party. If you lived in St James's, as we did, the hill down St James's Street was a splendid show of the 'spanking tits';* no interfering traffic, and only a hat-raising or bowing to friends hurrying up or down to their luncheon engagements.

Late afternoon in Hyde Park meant state carriages and barouches with beautifully dressed occupants pulled up under the trees. It was not etiquette to handle the reins oneself in afternoons, so we sat on rows of chairs chatting and behaving as if the world we knew bounded by the Smart Set was a fixed orbit, as if London—our London—was a place of select social enjoyment for the Circle, as if nothing could change in this best of delightful worlds. Then there would be clatter of faster horses, and down this mile of drive came the well-known Royal carriage with the beautiful Alexandra, Princess of Wales, bowing right and left as only she could bow, and hats were raised and knees curtsied before seats were resumed and interrupted chatter continued.

Hyde Park's day started early, with the early morning riders, who rode more for the exercise than as a social obligation. At home these people rode continually; the exercise was more necessary than ever here in the Season, with so many enormous meals to be shaken down. The early morning was probably the only time of day when you could enjoy a ride worthy of the name: it was all very well for the American commentator Richard Harding Davis to observe that 'The Row, with six hundred horses on it, is one of the finest sights of this show city', but 600 horses on that single strip of ground wouldn't provide much freedom of movement or opportunity to give your horse its head.

As the Countess of Warwick indicates, there were two fashionable periods in the Park. The first was the couple of hours or so before lunch, when what has been termed 'the biggest horse show in the world' could be seen. The Park was thronged with people, and the best parts of the Park were thronged with the best people. Charles Eyre Pascoe wrote in 1890:

Rotten Row is the entrance-way of the London fashionable world. Nowhere else is the assemblage so aristocratic, so little diluted with the streams of inferior humanity. Shabbiness never ventures here. Seated in one of the chairs along 'the Row' at the proper hour of the day, one may catch a glimpse of the most notable people in London; now of a Cabinet

---

* The oldest usage of this word is to signify a horse.

minister; now of a famous ambassador or foreign prince; now of a popular bishop; now of a leading radical MP; now of the Prince of Wales and his sons; now of a City magnate and ruler of the financial world; now of some famous artist, actor or popular author. The dress of the riders is faultless as the horses they ride. For aught one can see in Rotten Row on a midsummer morning, all the world may be prosperous, dignified, well-tailored and well-groomed. There is no such thing as poverty, and no such thing as work—all the world is bent on pleasuring.

Opposite *Views of Hyde Park*. ILN, *1889, and* Graphic, *1876*

At this hour of the day the carriages were chiefly the smaller varieties—tilburies, pony-chaises, four-in-hands—often driven by their owners who were well experienced in 'handling the ribbons'. Men and women—even gentlemen and their ladies—were no less proud of their vehicles then than are their descendants today, and no doubt there were many tedious discussions as to the relative merits of this or that harness, this or that type of springing.

Those who did not ride or drive would either sit or stroll on the pre-ordained strips of grass selected by Society. Formerly, the north side of the Row had been the more fashionable; by the late 1890s the preference had swung, for no clear reason, to the south. Custom and etiquette still controlled behaviour in the Park, though they were less restrictive here than elsewhere. True, a lady would not customarily ride alone in the Park at any hour of the day, but she was permitted a wide choice of companions. She would not normally ride alone with a young man, unless she was engaged to marry him. If two ladies rode on their own, they would probably be accompanied by a groom.

After lunch and the afternoon's engagements, the Park once again came into fashion, this time for the evening drive. In the words of Richard Harding Davis (*Harpers Magazine*, 1893):

The next step is to the Park in time to see the parade of carriages, which is possibly less interesting than the people who gather to look at it. Fashion has moved slowly but surely from west of Hyde Park Corner to Stanhope Gate, and has left its original gathering-ground to country cousins and foreigners, who sit like people in the theatre, clutching the little penny ticket which entitles them to a seat, gazing open-eyed at the procession of fine horses and haughty ladies and still haughtier coachmen.

The smart people haunted the lawn opposite Stanhope Gate last year, and that they were left to themselves and that no one not of their class came to stare at them is one of the curious facts that an American cannot understand. The Lawn opposite Stanhope Gate is as free as the air to anyone who pays his penny for a green chair, but no one not of a certain class goes there. They sit below, recognising an invisible barrier; they would not be comfortable opposite Stanhope Gate. This indefinable and unwritten right of the upper class to keep to itself is very interesting. Under that tree the Duchess of —— always sat, in this corner of the iron railing one was always sure to find the American heiress, and in the angle of the railing the Hon. Mrs —— held her court and received her devotees. No one reserved these places, and yet everyone recognised their right to them . . . The spot opposite Stanhope Gate looked more like a private lawn party than a public park.

The Party That Lasted 100 Days

The carriages were larger at this hour of the day, and driven by grooms, whose expert management was necessary in the crush. Barouches, victorias and state carriages proceeded slowly, halting frequently, while their occupants bowed or raised their hats to friends and acquaintances in other carriages or lining the way: or, less often, feigning not to recognise that a passing carriage carried a husband's mistress, a vulgar actress, or a pushing member of the nouveaux riches who was doing her damnedest to get into your good books.

For Hyde Park was useful not only to those who were securely 'in'; it was of crucial importance to those who were not quite in, or only just in by the skin of their teeth. They might not be invited to the best houses, they might not be able to mingle with the truly great in the privacy of their own homes, but here at least all were on common ground. As a *Harpers* correspondent observed:

> This period is one of great importance to young ladies not regularly in society, who have to utilise as far as possible the opportunity of contact with it. A chair in the Park on a fine evening is very favourable to business.

Hyde Park was particularly useful on Sundays, which as we have already noted was an awkward time of the week to fill. Here, every Sunday throughout the Season, and most particularly on the Sunday after Ascot, the best people gathered for the

Du Maurier,
Punch, *1888*

A COMBINATION OF AGREEABLES.

SATURDAY AFTERNOON—WEST WIND AND SUNSHINE—ROOM FOR ONE, SAY, TO HURLINGHAM AND BACK, OR ANYWHERE YOU LIKE

1888.

*An evening
walk in Hyde
Park.*
ILN, *1890*

'Prayer-book Parade', a spectacle which moved one observer, Montagu Williams,
to moralise in 1892:

> Not an uninteresting place during the Season is the Row on a Sunday morning. You see
> some curious sights there. Whether the people who carry prayer-books have all been to
> a place of worship I cannot say. To judge by their doings, I should think it rather doubtful.
> Here can be seen youth that has been sacrificed to age. It is true, you are told that that old
> gentleman—some noble earl, it may be—is devotedly attached to his fair young companion,
> and that she returns his affection. Well, it doesn't look much like it, to judge by the way
> she gazes wistfully around, heedless of the nonsense he is pouring into her ear . . .

Inevitably, as one reads one of these accounts after another, one builds up a
picture of Hyde Park as a place where the sun was always shining on gorgeous ladies
in gorgeous dresses, chatting with immaculate men in faultlessly styled suits, turning
only to watch as gleaming horses drew elegant carriages at a leisurely pace beneath
the trees. Nobody speaks of Hyde Park in the wind and the rain, under leaden skies
or damp with summer mists—and yet how often in reality that is how it must have
been. At such times it was not Society's Park, for this was part of a private dream-
world, artificially created by excluding whatever spoilt the picture or distressed the

Hyde Park.
Cassells, *1891*

spirits. And so, just as in the life of Society there was no shabbiness and no poverty, so in Society's Park the sun was indeed forever shining:

The Drive.
Doré, London,
1870

We pass over the shoulder of the Green Park to Hyde Park and the Ride [Douglas Jerrold writes]; and here are only the gently born and gently nurtured, driving the heat and faintness of the ballroom out, by spirited canters through a grove of such green leaves as only our well-abused English climate can produce.

Hyde Park at the height of the Season, Hyde Park on an afternoon when the Four-in-Hand Club is out in full force, is the best picture we can present to the stranger of the pride and wealth, the blood and bearing, the comeliness, beauty and metal of old England.

In the park are the grand headquarters of fashion that are not to be matched for stateliness, variety, and natural beauty—and where all the loveliness seen on drawing-room nights at the Opera, is to be met betimes gathering fresh roses amid the greenery.

Chapter 6
EATING AND DRINKING

Any activity which was conducive to 'togetherness' was welcomed by Society, and particularly was this true of the various mealtimes which stood like milestones along the course of the day. Society ate a colossal amount, even making allowance for the quantity of energy they must have burned up in their non-stop round of activity. Let us accompany them from one meal to the next:

BREAKFAST

For most people this was a private affair, and no vast quantities of food were put away. Here are some of Mrs Beeton's suggestions for what she terms 'the comfortable meal called breakfast': Broiled fish, mutton chops and rump-steaks, broiled sheep's kidneys, sausages, bacon and poached eggs, omelets, muffins, toast and marmalade etc . . .

Occasionally a hostess would decide to throw a breakfast party, and the meal became more formal—with fish, entrées, game and cold viands being given, accompanied by tea, coffee and liqueurs. Etiquette was informal—there was no taking in of partners as at dinner; instead, the hostess simply led the way into the dining room, followed first by the ladies and then by the gentlemen, with the host bringing up the rear. Eggs, potted meats and fish would be placed up and down the table, interspersed with racks of dry toast, hot rolls, teacakes and muffins, small loaves of brown and white bread, and dainty pats of butter within the reach of everyone. The more substantial dishes—such as hams, tongues and pies—were placed on the side-board. The gentlemen would often help the ladies and themselves. Hot dishes, such as kidneys, mushrooms and fried bacon, would be placed on the table.

Manners and Rules of Good Society offers some suggestions for summer breakfast dishes:

buttered eggs	veal cake	broiled whiting	beefsteak pie
potted shrimps	pigeons in jelly	devilled chicken	strawberries and raspberries

Eating And Drinking

Guests would normally leave the house as soon as breakfast was over, unless otherwise requested.

LUNCHEON

As late as 1894, Lady Colin Campbell could start her notes on lunch parties with an apology: 'Luncheon has been defined as an insult to one's breakfast and an outrage to one's dinner.' But to Society there were other things more important than the stomach; if lunch could be made to provide an opportunity for social intercourse, then let there be lunch parties—and Lady Campbell had to admit that they seemed to have come to stay.

Lunch was very much the ladies' meal. Not that they especially wanted it that way, but men tended to be otherwise occupied at this hour of the day—or else to have breakfasted so late that they were not ready to tackle another full meal at midday. So the presence of a gentleman visitor at the lunch table was considered an acquisition, and a hostess who could achieve a properly balanced party for this meal had a right indeed to be pleased with herself. So much was this the case that, while ladies usually expected to be invited to lunch in a formal fashion, many hostesses issued carte blanche to their male acquaintance, to invite themselves to lunch whenever they pleased.

Du Maurier,
Punch, c. *1890*

A LITTLE LUNCHEON AT TIMMINS'.

Host. "MAY I GIVE YOU SOME ROAST HARE, LADY JONES?"
Master Tommy (Lady Jones's Godson). "AH! I SAW COOK PEEL THAT CAT!"

The customary hour for lunch was 2 p.m., and you were expected to arrive within 10 minutes of the specified time. Ladies did not remove their hats or jackets, and strict precedence was not formally observed. The meal itself was either formal or informal, depending on the preference of the hostess. Sometimes the entire meal was served by the domestic staff; sometimes they handed the first course, then left the rest to the party; sometimes the guests helped themselves throughout. The same casualness applied to the way in which the meal was eaten. Lady Campbell tells us that 'it is quite allowable to push on one side the plate on which you have had tart or jelly, and take another before you with fruit or cheese. An elegant disorder is perfectly distinct from a vulgar confusion'—an epigram worth treasuring.

Opinions differed as to how long the meal should last. *Manners and Rules of Good Society* suggests that the whole affair should last only 30 to 45 minutes, and the guests be out of the house soon after 3 p.m. at the latest; but others preferred to make more of the occasion, stretching lunch through the afternoon to 4 p.m. and later.

As to what one ate, Lady Campbell suggests:

Any of the following may be selected for the luncheon table: Cold lamb, Pigeon, Pork or Beefsteak Pies, Pressed or Roasted Beef, Tongue, Fowls (boiled or roasted), Game, Veal patties, Potted meats, Lobsters, Salad, Fruit tarts, Light puddings, Custard, Stewed fruit, Jelly, Blancmange, Cheesecakes, Tartlets, Sponge or plum cake, Cheese, Biscuits, Butter and Fruits. The beverages offered should be sherry, claret, claret cup and light beer.

(It is perhaps worth remarking that that is the first and only mention of beer in these pages.)

AFTERNOON 'AT HOMES'

Afternoon entertaining, like lunch, could vary between the formal and the informal. Sometimes the refreshment offered by a hostess to her visitors would be purely a token—a cup of tea and a cucumber sandwich, say. But if it was a formal 'at home' with proper invitations, she would be expected to make more of an effort.

Manners and Rules tells us:

Afternoon 'at homes' are a great feature among the entertainments of the day, parties so large that the number of guests equals those at a big crush or evening reception, and so small that they might fairly come under the denomination of afternoon teas.

Ladies are present in considerable majority, there being usually from about ten gentlemen to thirty ladies on an average. Ladies have a decided partiality for this class of entertainment, as it offers an opportunity for meeting their friends and acquaintances, and for forming future plans and interchanging civilities—and even in the height of the London Season, afternoon 'at homes' are fully attended by the members of the fashionable world.

Eating And Drinking

And the same authority classifies the various categories in terms of the entertainment offered. Large 'at homes', where between 50 and 200 guests were invited, would often be favoured with professional vocal and instrumental talent, only just short of a fully-fledged concert. At smaller gatherings of less than a hundred, there would be music, but the performers were more likely to be amateurs; at gatherings with less than 30 guests, there would be no organised entertainment. Occasionally, but not often in London, there would be dancing.

The refreshments at a large 'at home' would be served in the dining room, on a long buffet. A typical menu would be:

Gelées aux Fruits
Crêmes variées

GLACES
Crême de Fraises
Eau de Muscat
Café Glacé

Limonade

Thé (chaud)
Gâteaux et Biscuits

Five o'clock tea.
1884

Another expert also recommends sherry, champagne cup, claret cup in addition to tea and coffee served from large silver urns. Coming an hour or two after a lunch party, and only three hours before the monumental dinners of the period, it sounds sufficiently substantial to keep the wolf from the door.

GARDEN PARTIES

From the refreshment point of view, a garden party was comparable to an 'at home' except that, having demanded more from your guests since such parties were frequently held at a distance from the West End, you were expected to give more in return. Tents of various picturesque shapes would be erected at suitable intervals throughout the grounds, in which refreshments were available for the guests to be served with a minimum of effort. Tea, coffee and cakes would be waiting for the guests when they arrived, and later these would be followed by suitable food and drink — ices, claret-cup, strawberries, grapes, melons and the like.

A garden party. London Magazine, *1904*

'The present fashion,' Lady Colin Campbell informs her readers, 'is to wear morning dress, but as picturesque as you please; indeed, the ladies should look like butterflies fluttering about. The men wear frock-coats, either dark-blue, grey or black, white waistcoats, light trousers, and silk hats.'

Eating And Drinking

Garden parties began about 4 p.m., and unless mention was specifically made of dancing, guests would be expected to leave between 7 and 8 p.m. Though their hostess received them on their arrival, they were not obliged to bid her farewell on leaving.

DINNER

It has often perplexed me to imagine how an Englishman will be able to reconcile himself to any future state of existence from which the earthly institution of Dinner shall be excluded.

(Nathaniel Hawthorne, *Our Old Home*)

Dinner was incomparably the most important meal of the day, as it was also the most substantial. A hostess was judged more by her dinner parties than by any of her other forms of hospitality; the composition of a well-balanced guest list was the greatest challenge to her skill and diplomacy. What sleepless nights must have been spent by aspiring hostesses, endeavouring to compose a party of dinner guests which

On the road to dinner. London Society, *1865*

would bring her public credit as well as private gratification!

Invitations were sent out at least three weeks in advance—sometimes as much as six weeks ahead, so as to make sure you got the guests you wanted. Invitations should be accepted or refused within 24 hours.

The dinner hour varied between 8 and 9 p.m.; 8.30 was the most usual time. Guests were expected to arrive 15 minutes after the stated hour, and dinner was served within 20 minutes of the arrival of the first guest. The host and hostess waited to receive their guests in the drawing room; at large parties the butler announced each new arrival. Hands would be shaken, the ladies would sit. No drinks were offered. The host would tell each gentleman which lady he was to take in, and introductions would be made. Dinner would be announced by the butler or a man-servant. The host would lead the way, taking in the senior lady present. The guests would follow in order of the ladies' precedence—with which it was of course the hostess's duty to be fully informed. She herself would go in last, with the senior male guest.

At the table, cards might be waiting in each place, or names might be written on the cover of the menus. There would be a menu to each guest or pair of guests, usually in holders, and written in French. At most formal dinner-parties the food was served *à la Russe*—that is to say, from a side table. The only exceptions would be the bowls of fruit left on the table at the end of the meal.

The menu would generally consist of eight or nine courses, roughly as follows:

> Soup (choice)
> Fish (choice)
> Entrées (choice of brown and choice of white)
> Removes (joint of meat or sometimes simple vegetables)
> Poultry and/or game
> Sweets (choice)
> Cheese
> Ices
> Fruit

Here are two typical menus, the first for spring and the second for summer, suggested by Lady Colin Campbell, each for twelve guests:

SOUP

Asparagus   Vermicelli

FISH

Salmon   Plain Whitebait   Devilled Whitebait

ENTREES

Beef Olives   Quenelles of Rabbit
Lobster Cutlets   Reform Cutlets

Eating And Drinking

REMOVES

Quarter of Lamb　　　　Capon, with Ham

Green Peas

GAME

Quails　　　　Plovers

SWEETS

Iced soufflé　　　　　　　　Fruit jelly

Pineapple Cream　　　　　Gooseberry Tart

Ramekins　　　　　　　Russian Salad

ICES

Vanilla Cream　　　　Orange Water

FRUITS

Strawberries　　　Cherries　　　Melons

SOUP

Oxtail　　　Bisque

FISH

Salmon　　　Smelts

ENTREES

Curried Eggs　　　　Sweetbreads and mushrooms

Vol au vent à la Financière

REMOVES

Iced asparagus

GAME

Quails　　　　　　Larks (July)

Grouse　　　　Black Cock (Aug–Sept)

Partridges

SWEETS

Ice pudding　　　　　　　Strawberry Jelly

Confiture of nectarines　　　Iced Meringues

Cheese Straws　　　Cheese　　　Butter

ICES

Neapolitan Cream　　　Raspberry Water

FRUIT

Pineapples　　　　　　Strawberries

Cherries　　　　　　Apricots

Melons

71

Above
*A formal
dinner party.*
Fred Barnard,
ILN, c. *1870*

THINGS ONE WOULD RATHER HAVE LEFT UNSAID.   1886.

Host (across table). "BY THE WAY, BISHOP, I HEAR SIR WORMWOOD AND LADY SCRUBBS ARE IN TOWN, AND JUSTICE TUPPER AND HIS WIFE. I ONLY WISH I HAD KNOWN IT BEFORE, FOR I WOULD HAVE ASKED THEM TO-DAY TO MEET YOU!"

Mental Chorus of Guests. "I WONDER WHICH OF US WOULD HAVE BEEN LEFT OUT!"

Left
Du Maurier,
Punch, *1886*

Eating And Drinking

The point of offering so many dishes was to suit all tastes; no guest was expected to work his way through the entire menu, though it was perfectly permissible for him to do so. The servants would offer each dish in turn to each guest in turn, who would help himself or refuse as he wished. It was not done to ask for a second helping of any dish.

The wine drunk with dinner was nearly always claret; diners of the period seem to have had relatively unsophisticated palates. Indeed, the Prince of Wales had so marked a preference for champagne that it became fashionable at some tables to serve this throughout the meal, to the extent that in certain circles the word 'wine' was taken to imply champagne and no other.

At the end of the meal the ladies, led by the hostess, would retire from the table. They would gather in the drawing-room, where coffee was served at once, frequently accompanied by crystallised ginger. Coffee was also taken in to the gentlemen, who would sit drinking and smoking for a while, usually moving to seats close to their host. Contrary to modern belief, it was not usual for the men to stay long by themselves—15 or 20 minutes was the rule.

After joining the ladies, the men would no longer smoke, though this rule lapsed during the Edwardian period. Tea would be served fairly soon after the coffee; then at about 10.30 p.m. the guests would leave, the butler announcing each carriage as it arrived.

For the inexperienced, a dinner party was a formidable affair. Apart from matters of precedence and the awkwardness felt by any Englishman or woman on being introduced, there were important points such as remembering which arm to hand to your partner (answer: the gentleman offered his right arm). Then, at the table, other problems cropped up—translating the menu, deciding which dish to choose, knowing how to eat some of the more awkward dishes, coping with the cutlery, disposing of cherrystones. Fortunately, there were many handy books of etiquette, often written by Members of the Aristocracy or The Gentleman in the Club Window, which served as guides among the shoals and quicksands of the dinner table. Here are a few of their more curious hints:

It is etiquette to start eating as soon as a dish is set before you.

Soup is eaten out of a plate, and with a spoon.

Peas should be eaten with a fork.

In eating asparagus, a knife and fork should be used, and the points should be cut off and eaten with a fork.

Young ladies do not eat cheese, nor game, nor savouries. [This must have been because such dishes might be supposed to mar their breath.]

When eating grapes, the half-closed hand should be placed to the mouth, and the fore-finger curved above the mouth in a manner which serves to conceal the ejectment of the skin and seeds, which are allowed to fall into the fingers and conveyed to the plate, the fingers being afterwards wiped with the napkin.

Jellies should be eaten with a fork.

When eating cheese, small morsels should be placed with the knife on small morsels of bread, and the two conveyed to the mouth with the thumb and finger, the piece of bread being the morsel to hold. Cheese should not be eaten off the point of the knife.

Preserved ginger is eaten with the knife and fork.

Apples and pears, peaches and apricots, are peeled with the knife and fork.

Bananas are peeled with the knife and fork, and the pieces are conveyed to the mouth by means of the fork.

Let me advise you to avoid embarking on an orange, unless you are an adept. It requires

long experience, a colossal courage, any amount of cool self-possession, and a great skill, to attack and dispose of one without harm to yourself or your neighbour.

RESTAURANT MEALS

Restaurant and hotel meals were of course a necessity for travellers, but until the closing years of the nineteenth century Society saw no reason to make a social occasion of them. Bachelors, tired of their clubs, might gather in a restaurant and take lady friends who would not be admitted within the portals of Society; but in general the best people preferred to eat in one another's houses, and despised the restaurant except in cases of necessity.

But in the 1890s the situation changed, and with remarkable rapidity. A lady journalist who called herself 'Madge' of *Truth* magazine commented:

> The development of restaurant life in London proceeds apace. To dine out three or four nights a week at some of the palatial establishments is not unusual, and that, too, in a grade of society that was one of the most domestic order. Perhaps the general unsatisfactoriness of cooks has something to do with it. It used to drive a man to his club. Now it drives him and his wife to a restaurant.

The author of *The Night Side of London* enlarges:

> Men don't dine at their clubs nowadays; they go with their wives or the wives of others to partake of the Restaurant Dinner. These Restaurant Dinners are comparatively recent institutions, having come into vogue during the last few years, but they have become almost, if not altogether, the greatest feature of the Night Side of London high life. Fashion shifts about a bit amongst the larger restaurants, and there are certain of them more frequented by one smart set than another. But all, or nearly all, the big hotels have restaurants, and some of the smaller, and perhaps a trifle more select, have them too; they cater handsomely for tout le monde that can pay. So you may dine at Claridge's, or the Carlton, or the Cecil, or the Savoy, or if you prefer a restaurant pure and simple, at Prince's, the Imperial, the Trocadero, the Criterion, Frascati's, and so forth. No shade of doubt but you get the best dinners in London at the restaurants, and see the most interesting company in them as well.

The reasons for the change were several: first, those already alluded to—a decline in the quality and availability of cooks; fewer people maintained establishments capable of providing sufficiently sophisticated fare. Secondly, restaurants were particularly convenient on such occasions as theatre visits, when a party could dine at an establishment next door to the theatre and move from dinner-table to box without haste.

A third reason was that restaurants were 'neutral ground'—you could meet there without incurring any of the obligations of hospitality in your own home, with all the delicacy of status and protocol, calls and card-leaving, which this involved. Dining at a restaurant was a simple commercial transaction, and many people found this a welcome relief after the strain of giving and receiving hospitality within Society.

A final reason for taking to the restaurant was the good value if afforded. Here, for example, is what the Grand Hotel at Charing Cross offered by way of table d'hôte for five shillings:

NATIVE OYSTERS

POTAGES
Croûte au Pot
Crême à la Persanne

POISSONS
John Dory à la Bercy
Filets de Soles à la Horly

ENTREE
Pigeonneaux à la Paysanne

RELEVES
Sirloin of Beef
Jambon glacé au Porto

LEGUMES
Champignons Sautés
Pommes de Terre Croquettes

ROTI
Faisans Bardés

ENTREMETS
Abricots en Cassolettes
Gâteaux Victoria

DESSERT
Bombes de Melons
Fruits Assortis

It will be seen that the French language had already established itself on English menus just as French cuisine had imposed itself on English palates. No other kind of ethnic food seems to have been available in respectable London—not even the now ubiquitous Italian restaurants, let alone Chinese, Indian or Turkish, though there were places in the East End where the venturesome gastronome might find anything he wanted.

By and large it does not seem that people in Society were particularly interested

in food as food. Meals were an excuse for social gathering, and while people liked the food served to be pleasing to palate and to eye, they did not take it as seriously as did their neighbours across the Channel. Similarly with restaurants: their greatest virtue was their convenience. They gave a lady the chance to eat out while shopping; Pascoe's *London of Today* for 1890 lists a number of eating places in Regent Street and Piccadilly where ladies might lunch on their own and be tolerably sure of a 'cutlet, very nicely served'. There were tea-shops of delightful daintiness, some with music to accompany the cakes and ices; and there were even Dorothy restaurants which catered exclusively for ladies and admitted no gentlemen whatever.

Chapter 7
EVENING PARTIES

Evening parties came in an infinite variety of shapes and sizes, but fell into two main groups—those at which the guests danced, and those at which they didn't.

If they didn't, the party was known formally as a reception, more colloquially as a kettledrum or, simpler still, a drum. A reception was the usual type of party offered by official hostesses—the wives of ambassadors and politicians acting in their public capacity.

Arriving for a party. Graphic, *1897*

After the ball the commonest form of 'fashionable arrangement' is the drum, or evening reception. This is less expensive, and involves less trouble in the way of house cleaning. These considerations bring it within the reach of everyone and in consequence the drum

Evening Parties

An aristocratic reception. Du Maurier, Graphic, 1888

presents more varieties than any other species of entertainment. The *grand monde* and his wife, and everybody else and their wives, may be at a drum, or it may be a forlorn gathering, with half a dozen women seated together, and half a dozen men eyeing them from afar off. A drum may display a rich banquet, for supper, or a table bearing biscuits and barley-water. But there is this consolation—everyone can leave when he likes, a step that is not always possible at a ball.

There is not the slightest idea of harmonious intercourse present in the mind of a drum-giver. Anyone she knows, or thinks she knows, is invited in the order in which the names stand in the 'red book'.* The accepted conditions of most drums, however, make it unnecessary to consider the possibility of intimate or congenial society. The dearest friends might miss each other in the throng, or be unable to greet except over the bodies of their fellow-creatures. The main object of going is to get away. The young and strong plunge in at one end, and come out at the other looking as if they had waded through a torrent. The older persons hang about in eddies and backwaters until they can work their way to the door. These are the drawbacks of the drum. On the other hand, it has this advantage—that persons can be met there who do not frequent the gayer forms of amusement.

As the anonymous *Harpers* correspondent suggests, the main object of attending

---

* *Burke's Peerage*, which lists the aristocracy in strict order of precedence, is always bound in red.

Going down to supper at a ball. Graphic, 1890

a reception was to be able to say that you had been there. Consequently the status of the hostess and host was the vital factor. However tedious it might be, a reception given by one of the reigning 'queens' of Society was an engagement to be sought after, even if you only attended it for a matter of minutes—simply to be able to sport the invitation on your mantelshelf was a feather in your social cap. A smart reception in a big house was a splendid affair in appearance, moreover; those who did not possess imposing enough premises of their own would frequently rent or borrow someone else's house for the occasion.

The hour of invitation varied between 10 and 11 p.m.—the more intimate affairs starting at the earlier hour, the more distinguished at the later; this applied to official receptions in particular. When someone of special importance was to be present, the words 'to meet So-and-So' would be written on the card.

Guests were expected to arrive between 30 and 90 minutes of the hour mentioned on the invitation. Tea and light refreshments were served throughout the evening in the library or some other convenient room, and it was usual to provide some kind of formal entertainment, such as professional vocal or instrumental music. Supper was served about 12 p.m., and was similar to the ball supper which will be described later in this chapter; supper marked the end of the proceedings, and guests would go from the supper-room to leave without returning to the party or taking formal leave

'Ten shillings a night! The fair player turns with a wistful glance'. London Society, *1865*

of their host and hostess. On Saturdays receptions ended at midnight, so that arrival and supper times would need to be brought forward.

Dancing parties, too, came in various forms. To start with, there was a distinction between a 'ball' proper, and a mere 'dance'. The invitation did not directly indicate this distinction—all such functions were styled dances—but the differences were real enough. At a dance the number of guests was between 80 and 200; at a ball it was between 200 and 500. At a dance the music might be provided by a pianist; at a ball there was always a full band. At a dance there were few or no floral decorations; at a ball these would be numerous and costly.

In Town, Ball giving is in a way a science, and an amusement upon which large sums of money are frequently expended. The selection of night is of paramount importance, as when a smarter ball is given at a smarter house on the particular evening chosen by the giver of a less brilliant ball, the grander ball extinguishes the lesser ball, through the most fashionable people merely looking in at the one, and remaining the rest of the evening at the other. The guests who had been expected to add lustre to the lesser ball appear but for a few minutes, and usually arrive rather early—uncomplimentarily early, perhaps a little before eleven—and remain hardly half an hour in the rooms, making their way to another ball of the same calibre, and remaining there perhaps another twenty minutes, before arriving at the goal, viz. *the* ball of the evening. Thus, at a little after twelve, an average ball giver finds her rooms deserted by all but those who have nowhere else to go.

(*Manners and Rules of Good Society*)

A little hop in Harley Street. Du Maurier, London Society, *1863*

Such a dismal occasion might be a failure insofar as the party itself was concerned,

but did not necessarily imply a social failure—for everyone would understand the situation, and credit would still be marked up to the lesser hostess for giving her party at all. Nevertheless, popular or not, these smaller dances were often fairly dreadful affairs:

The ordinary dwellings of the metropolis contain, for the purpose of receiving guests, rooms of the same pattern. Of course the size varies, but the usual type is a front room more or less oblong, and a back room more or less square, communicating with the former by folding doors. This inevitable setting gives to most balls a certain similarity, and usually, from its narrow dimensions, prevents them, however eligible in other ways, from attaining the excellence of a ball in a 'big house'.

There is always the hostess with her daughter at the top of the stairs, surrounded by a crowd who have bowed or shaken hands with that lady, and who afterward appear as if they were trying to hide themselves from her and her offspring as fast as possible. The musicians are blockaded in one corner, and round the doors the black-coated young men cluster like bees in swarming time. Mothers and daughters are ranged two or three deep round the walls, the more fortunate of the former sitting, but many on foot.

In the middle of the room, reduced to an irregular space of about ten feet by six, struggling couples beat one against another. On their faces are expressed various emotions —high spirits and depression, malice and good humour, pleasure and pain. The floor oscillates; wax candles sprinkle their substance liberally about; hot young men open windows, and chilly dowagers shut them. Now and then a black coat detaches itself from the mass near the door, and with a patronising air selects a partner, or makes a few gracious observations to a chaperon. Everything is sound and tumult, the only approach to repose being on the back stairs, where two or three couples sit in a blissful state watching other couples wedge their way to the tea-room through opposing masses who press back to the dancing. In the tea-room is a still denser throng, above which arms are raised waving tea-cups, glasses of lemonade, ices, and other light refreshments.

Behind the buffet the upper female servants, with a hired waiter to touch up, thrust anything they can reach into the hands of the innumerable suppliants. Later on, when supper is announced, the stress of the fight is transferred to the dining-room. A new element in the shape of the hungry and irritated chaperon now mingles in the fray. This imports a seriousness into what was before half playful, and most of the younger and more timid withdraw from all attempts to obtain food. The remainder squeeze themselves round small tables, or stand, disconsolate, eyeing the expanse of heads for a vacant space. The butler and footmen look haughtily round them, while hirelings feed the guests. And so the battle proceeds until about three in the morning, when it probably turns into a ball, and the survivors enjoy themselves until broad daylight.

(*Harpers*, 1886)

At the height of the Season, three or four balls were given every night; more often than not, they probably corresponded to the above description. But certain houses had a greater cachet, and consequently so did the balls they gave. The same writer makes the comparison:

In the case of a ball at one of the big houses, things are more elegant and more comfortable.

Evening Parties

What a contrast, for instance, is the arrival! Instead of a ladder filled with a mass of persons heaving slowly upward, a stately staircase winds round a large hall. Masses of flowers form a background to women's forms bright with diamonds, magnificent with brocatelle and lace, or fair with the freshness of youth in a cloud of tulle. On the broad steps slowly ascending groups dispose themselves picturesquely, the trains of the gowns trailing over the low steps. Above, behind balustrades and pillars of marble, other guests sit watching the arrivals. Large rooms, the walls hung with historic pictures, open out of each other in long vistas. Perhaps two or three of these will be cleared for dancing, but the others will be left in their everyday state of comfort, where non-dancers can stroll or sit as luxuriously as if no ball was going on. There is probably a terrace, balcony or garden, lit with Chinese lamps, where those who are hot can breathe a cooler air. The whole festival is full of colour, richness and life, and, were it not for the black coats, quite a Venetian scene.

Etiquette at a dance or a ball was more formalised than at almost any other type of function. The hostess stood at the head of the staircase to receive her guests, and shook hands with each as he or she arrived. The dancing was opened either by the hostess herself or by one of her daughters, the gentleman of highest rank present dancing the first quadrille with her. Gentlemen were expected to dance at least once with the daughters of the house; clearly at a big ball this wasn't possible, but they should nevertheless make the offer.

Opposite
Flirtation versus dancing.
Graphic, *1876*

Below
'*May I have the pleasure?*'
c. *1890*

Evening Parties

Dance programmes, though still used in the country, were no longer used in London in the 1890s. The dances in vogue were as follows:

Opposite *The first quadrille, and the last galop.* ILN, *1873*

> Quadrille
> Lancers
> Valse
> Highland Schottische
> Highland Reel
> Polka (replacing the formerly popular Galop)
> Cotillon (with which the ball closed; some hostesses gave
>   costly presents to the guests in the course of this dance).

An unmarried girl would not attend a dance without being chaperoned by a married woman or some other female companion who had supposedly reached years of discretion, and whose respectability (a chaperon was originally a kind of cloak) protected the girl against any hint of impropriety.

A girl should not dance more than three times with any one partner. Though she would not necessarily be returned by her partner to her chaperon after each dance, she should not, however great the temptation, make it difficult for herself to be found by her next promised partner—though doubtless this frequently occurred.

The American Richard Harding Davis noticed some interesting differences between the behaviour at dances of English girls and those of his own country:

Punch, c. *1890*

PUTTING HIS FOOT IN IT.

Kate. "I'M AFRAID YOU'RE ENTANGLED!"

Augustus. "DON'T CARE, I'M SURE—IF *YOU* DON'T."

Above left
'*Youth and
beauty at the
Whitehall
Rooms*'.
London of
today, *1890*

Above right
*Running repairs.
1883*

The dances in London, at the first glance, are like smart dances in New York, as far as the young people and the music and the palms and the supper and such things go. There is, however, a very marked difference in the solemnity of the young men and in the shyness and sedateness of the young girls. There are certain interests to offset this, which are lacking with us, one of which is the number of married women you see whose faces are already familiar to you on both sides of the Atlantic through their photographs in shop windows, and who keep you wondering where you have come across them and their tiaras before, and another is the greater number of servants, whose livery and powdered hair add colour to the halls, and who, when they pass on the word that 'Lady Somebody's carriage blocks the way' are much more picturesque than Johnson in his ulster and high hat calling out '23 East Twenty-second Street'. There is a more brilliant showing of precious stones in London, and the older men in the sashes and stars of the different orders of the empire add something to the colour and distinction which we do not have at home. Otherwise the scene is much the same.

It is only when you leave the ballroom and go out onto the lawn or into the surrounding rooms that you come across an anomaly which is most disturbing. The American girl who seeks corners and the tops of stairways or who, when the weather permits, wanders away from the care of her chaperon and the lighted rooms into the garden round the house, is sure to suffer the penalty of being talked about. Young married women may do that sort

90

of thing with us, but a young girl must remain in evidence, she must be where her partners can reach her, and where whoever is looking after her can whisper to her to hold herself straight, or that she is dancing with her hair down.

If she wants to talk to a man alone, as she sometimes does, and her mother approves of the man, she can see him at her own home over a cup of tea any afternoon after five. But she cannot do this if she is an English girl in London. So when the English girl goes to a dance at a private house she takes advantage of the long waits between each dance, which are made very long on purpose, and rushes off, not only into rooms leading from the ballroom, but up stairs to the third and fourth storey, or out into the garden, where she sits behind statues and bushes, and so, when you wander out for a peaceful smoke, you are constantly intruding upon a gleaming shirt front and the glimmer of a white skirt hidden away in a surrounding canopy of green. It is most embarrassing.

Montagu Williams, an English man-about-town from an older generation, made the same observation, though his was a different point of view. Curiously, though, he does not appear to realise that his second paragraph may in some degree explain his first:

As for the balls and parties of society in the present day, they are nothing. Men don't dance now, at least the young men don't. It is too much of a bore, and it is always too hot. They prefer to 'sit out'. A man takes up a young girl for the evening, and they pass the time in quiet nooks and corners. What a change from the good old robust English society of fifty years ago!

It is at these entertainments that most of the marriages of the year are knocked up. I say 'knocked up' because that expression fittingly describes what takes place. It may be that some wretched girl has been hawked about for three or four seasons, and has come to be a drug in the matrimonial market. Her mother, who should be her protectress and well-wisher, is never tired of reproaching her. The cost of her dresses is thrown in her face, and she is constantly reminded that Lilian So-and-So and Gertrude So-and-So, without half her looks or figure, have married rent-rolls of thousands a year. At last the girl becomes callous, and, utterly regardless of all that should bring two hearts together, allows herself to be sold to the highest bidder, in nine cases out of ten not caring sixpence halfpenny for the bargain.

Guests generally came on to a ball after a dinner party at which, as we have seen, they had supped substantially enough to keep going till the next day's breakfast. Yet with appetites reawakened if not by dancing, then by battling to and from the buffet table, they demanded a steady provision of refreshment from the moment they arrived. As soon as hats and cloaks had been left in the cloakroom, the guests were shown into the refreshment room where, even before they had greeted their hostess, they could refresh themselves with tea or coffee, cakes and biscuits.

Similar light refreshments were available throughout the evening; after each dance, a gentleman would ask his partner if she would like a little something, and if she did, he would escort her to the refreshment room where two or three servants

'The missing
partner'.
ILN, *1871*

Opposite
'Number 10—
Lancers: Captain Fitz-
Sparkle'.
Bernard
Partridge,
ILN, *1892*

would be waiting with a selection of drinks—claret, champagne, cider, lemonade, sherry or coffee—accompanied by small cakes, biscuits and wafers, and ices.

All this was additional to the supper itself, to which the hostess would lead the way at about 1 a.m. Ladies would be taken to the supper-room by their partner from the previous dance. Here are Lady Campbell's suggestions for the supper buffet:

Flowers and fruits should occupy the middle of the table, from one end to the other. Bonbons, crackers, and ornamented cakes should spring up on all sides, together with frothy trifles, quivering jellies, snowy creams, and light soufflés, all placed in glass dishes. Then there are oyster patties, savoury jellies, lobster salads, veal cakes, and the more substantial dishes of cold salmon, game pie, boiled turkey, fowls boiled and roasted— these should have been carved before coming to table, and tied together in their original form with white satin ribbon, so that the person before whom they are placed has no further trouble than to untie the bow and put each piece on a plate as required. Hams, tongues and game, everything is cold at these suppers except soup, which is now often handed in cups. Neither vegetables nor cheese show themselves. Ices should be provided,

and the beverages are sherry, claret, light and sparkling wines, and the different kinds of cups, champagne being the greatest favourite.

'The supper'.
Du Maurier,
Harpers
Monthly, *1885*

Below
Musicians at
play. Hugh
Thomson,
English
Illustrated
Magazine,
1883

Evening Parties

The expense—both of money and of time and trouble—was obviously colossal. The anguish of the hostess can be imagined. Was it worthwhile? Only she, and her daughters, could answer that. Dances were, alas, more to the feminine taste than to the masculine: Montagu Williams's strictures quoted above were perfectly just, and the etiquette books of the period are strident in their appeals to young men to do their duty at dances, to repay their hostess by dancing instead of hanging about in the refreshment rooms. Here is the way such a ball seemed to bachelor guest Robert Machray:

Pray imagine you have been flattered by receiving an invitation to the Duchess of Blankshire's ball, and that you are now among her Grace's guests, of whom there are so many that it is somewhat difficult for you to get about. You came in excellent temper, for just before you started off, you remarked to your friends at the Club, who you knew had not been asked, with an irritatingly distinct voice, that you supposed you 'must go, though balls are such a bore'; you are therefore well aware that you are envied and sincerely detested by the men less fortunate than yourself—and this is to have succeeded! Each would like to tell you with conviction that your going to the ball, or your not going, won't make the slightest difference to anybody on earth, but they haven't the courage. So off you drive—perhaps a little after eleven o'clock—in high spirits, and very greatly tickled with yourself. You wait your turn in the street in the long line of carriages moving by fits and starts up to her Grace's door, and if your patience is not too severely tried, you will in time descend and walk under a red canopy brilliantly lit with many twinkling electric lamps into the hall, which is filled with flowers and flunkies, to say nothing of people like yourself arriving all the while, and is also brilliantly illuminated with pink and silver lights. Your fellow-guests wear a pleased look on top of their clothes; this is part of the game of manners.

Having deposited your hat and cape, you join the crowd on the great staircase, and push or are pushed upwards to shake her Grace by the hand. Should she happen to know you, you may get a word or two from her, but as it is much more likely that she hasn't the ghost of an idea who you are, you will pass silently by, and soon get lost in the crowd. It's a case of not being able to see the trees for the wood; one can't find one's friends in the crush—indeed, unless you are either very tall or particularly self-assertive, you may see hardly anybody.

It may be that you are a dancing man—a somewhat rare bird these days. Her Grace's ballroom is the finest in London, and the music is insinuating and inviting. You would if you could—but you can't. The floor is already covered, and movement is difficult. A few couples are really dancing, but the majority are mere revolving figures, confined within a narrow orbit; if they attempt to get outside of it their career is immediately stopped by more revolving couples, who frown down the eccentricity of the other dancers. This is how it is in the waltzes. Your Englishman does better in a romping polka or in a swinging barn-dance, for these are things in which brawn and muscle tell far more than skill, and the English girl has a weakness for brawn and muscle.

Having taken in so much of this, you perhaps come to the conclusion that the best way to enjoy a dance is to sit it out. So you take your partner and lead her out of the crush, and make for the stairs perhaps, or for some cosy nook or other where you may recover your breath, and say such things as are wont to be said on such occasions, wondering silently but persistently if you will be able to get any supper.

Supper is a matter of prime importance. Her Grace's mansion is a vast place, and the supper (if you can only get a chance to reach it) is sure to be excellent. But then her guests are legion: how are they all to be fed? If you are a really great personage, then of course you need have no misgivings. The Duchess will see that you are taken care of. But if you belong to the crowd of people who are not great in any way, it is just possible that you may have to scramble for your food—such things are not altogether unknown even at the Duchess of Blankshire's entertainments.

Still, in process of time you will be fed and you will have your thirst quenched. Then back for an hour or two in the ballroom again, or to some other part of the house. After what you assure her Grace with a vacuous smile has been such a pleasant evening, you go off again, at two or three in the morning, remarkably glad that it is all over.

But this is the jaded view of an Englishman, and it is characteristic of the English to run down the great and the splendid, however deeply they admire them in secret. Many men might laugh in agreement with Machray's description, but for all that they would be glad enough to be included on the Duchess's next invitation list— and that not only for the prestige involved. Despite the discomfort and the over-crowding, a big ball was a splendid affair; and it is only just to end this chapter with yet another quotation from an American witness—Richard Harding Davis—who managed to hold on to his illusions in spite of his concern for the morals of English girls:

The most novel feature of the dance in London is the sudden changing of night into day, at the early hour of two in the morning. Daylight obtrudes so late in New York that it is generally the signal for going home—but it comes so early in the game in London that one often sees the cotillon begun in a clear sunlight, which does not mar, but rather heightens the beauty of the soft English complexions and the fair arms and shoulders of the young girls, even while it turns the noblest son and heir of the oldest house present into something distressingly like a waiter . . .

This is one of the prettiest sights in London: a room full of young girls, the older women having discreetly fled before the dawn, romping through a figure in the smartest of décolleté gowns, and in the most brilliant sunlight, with the birds chirping violently outside, and the fairy-lamps in the gardens smoking gloomily, and the Blue Hungarian Band yawning over their fiddles.

Chapter 8

THEATRE AND OPERA

Beyond all doubt the amusement that delights the largest number of the cultivated in London is the opera. It is the quiet evening of the fagging pleasure week. The opera and then home, is an off-night which is delightful to the weary traveller from garden-party, to tea, to dinner, to conversazione, and rout, and ball—who has no rest from sunset to sunrise, and is then due in the Park in the morning. Or it is an hour's rest, before the fatigues of the night begin. 'As one cannot go to bed in the middle of the afternoon—11.30 p.m.—it is necessary to go somewhere after the opera' is the declaration of a well-known poseur on the subject. Without the opera, the pleasures of a London season would count its victims by the score. From the weariness of the round, the opera is the glorious and delightful rest. It is repose to the body and comfort to the mind.

(Jerrold, *London, A Pilgrimage,* 1872)

At the end of the nineteenth century there were 38 theatres in central London, together with many more in the outlying parts of the city and a great number of variety and music halls. All told, they amounted to 112 places of stage entertainment, which between them could cater for 80,000 patrons every night.

Needless to say, not all of these were patronised by Society—not even by Society in 'East End' mood, when for the gentlemen at any rate an evening at the 'halls' was considered a welcome change from more respectable amusements. But the theatre and the opera certainly had their place in Society's scheme of things. At first one might suppose that here, if anywhere, Society would be swallowed up in the public at large; the theatre was not exclusive to Society; anybody who could afford the price of a ticket might attend whatever spectacle he chose. And yet, even in this public domain, Society was able to dictate its own terms to a certain degree.

One example was the way in which Society hostesses would buy up all the best seats at the opera in advance. Lady So-and-So would have her own box for certain nights of the week—and if she did not choose to use it herself, she would offer it to friends. But even more significant is the fact that, though the theatrical season began in September and ran through to the following July, it was only in the last three months —that is to say, precisely those months which coincided with the Season proper— that evening dress was obligatory in the boxes, stalls and dress circles of the leading theatres.

Only a few decades before, the theatrical profession had been a despised one, and

Theatre dinner at the Hotel Métropole. London of today, *1889*

theatre-going not a popular diversion in Society. It was no coincidence that a famous journal of the period was entitled *The Sporting and Dramatic News*: even the most celebrated and admired actors and actresses were considered only the equal, socially speaking, of pugilists and champion pedestrians. But the status of the actor

Theatre And Opera

Stalls at the opera. Graphic, *1870*

Visiting a box. Graphic, *1894*

soared rapidly in the last three decades of the century; members of the profession were invited to the best houses, patronised by Royalty, even had titles bestowed on them. Photographs of celebrated actresses and matinée idols were displayed in shop windows—Victoria, visiting one of her sons during an illness, saw a photograph of Lily Langtry pinned over his bed (she removed it immediately with her own hands).

One of the reasons for the improved status of the actors and actresses was no doubt the improved quality of the material in which they appeared. Much of it, then as always, was rubbish; but at least it was generally now rubbish with some 'class' to it.

The smoking room at the opera.
Graphic, *1895*

And even if one held out against Ibsen and his kind, there were still excellent plays being written by writers like Pinero and Wilde—then as always, what the audience liked was plays about people like themselves, and Society was well served with 'problem' dramas about Society people. *The Second Mrs Tanqueray, Lady Windermere's Fan, The Notorious Mrs Ebbsmith*—such titles pulled in Society audiences as nothing else had ever done.

Picking a typical day more or less at random, one finds that in May 1890 the London theatregoer could choose, among others, these offerings:

> Lily Langtry in a new play, *Esther Sandraz*.
> Gilbert and Sullivan's *The Gondoliers* at the Savoy.
> *She Stoops to Conquer* at the Vaudeville.
> A season of French plays (in French) at Her Majesty's,
>   including Sarah Bernhardt as Joan of Arc.
> Henry Irving as Matthias in *The Bells*.
> Pinero's farce *The Cabinet Minister*.
> At the opera, *Carmen, Lohengrin* and *Faust*.

Theatre-going was frequently a matter of making up a party—Society liked to make a group-activity of everything it did in public, however secretive it might be in its more private doings. Dinner would need to be earlier and less leisurely than usual, for most plays began at 8.15 or 8.30 p.m.; however, it wasn't always necessary to get to the theatre for the start of the show, for some plays, such as the Lily Langtry item listed above, were scheduled to begin at 9 p.m., having been preceded by a short farce.

Theatre prices were relatively high; a box cost between 4 and 8 guineas, a seat in the stalls half a guinea. Behaviour at the theatre was not markedly different from that which still obtains today, merely more formal in appearance and less considerate in its attitude to the show and its performers. Refreshments were frequently carried round by attendants to the boxes, and sometimes to the stalls as well. It was however rare for ladies to eat or drink at the play.

The question of smoking cropped up in the etiquette books. A smoking foyer was found in all the best theatres, and would be frequented only by gentlemen. *Manners for Men* held strong opinions on the subject:

Between the acts of a play the modern man thinks it his duty to go out and have a drink, perhaps smoke a cigarette. But who shall say what golden opinions are won by those who do not follow the custom, who refrain from acquiring the odour of tobacco, or whiskey, or brandy, while they are in the company of ladies in the heated atmosphere of a theatre? A lady sometimes says to the man of the party, 'I see that there is a general stampede going on. Don't mind me if you would like to go out.' If they go, she thinks, 'Oh, they are just like the rest!' If they stay she says to her own heart, 'How delightful it is to find a man who can do without a brandy-and-soda or a smoke for two or three hours!' and up they go many pegs in her estimation.

Above left
*Eleonora Duse
in Pinero's
notorious* The
Second Mrs
Tanqueray.
ILN, *1900*

Above right
*Mrs Patrick
Campbell in
Pinero's no less
scandalous* The
Notorious
Mrs Ebbsmith.
Graphic, *1895*

Right
*Leaving the
Saint James's
Theatre after
a matinée.*
Living
London, *1900*

The opera was more closely linked with the Season than the drama. In 1890, for example, the opera season was spread over ten weeks from the middle of May to the end of July, coinciding closely with the Season itself. There were forty performances altogether, on Mondays, Tuesdays, Thursdays and Saturdays. Such was the popularity of the opera, however, that by the early 1900s the season had been stretched to some sixty performances.

The favourite operas remained the Italian ones—there was a general feeling that all good opera came from Italy, both the writing and the singing of it. Verdi was the grand old man of the business, then as now. But—against all prophecy—the German Wagner had come to stay; after his controversial initial impact on the musical world, his operas had become established items in the repertoire, and in the 1889 season at Covent Garden *Lohengrin* was the biggest single draw.

The cost of opera-going was extremely high. Prices were about twice what they were for the theatre—that is to say, a seat in the stalls cost a guinea (and even more on special nights) and a box from $2\frac{1}{2}$ to 8 guineas (much the same price range as at the theatre, but the average was higher). One would have to multiply this by about five to get anything like a present-day equivalent. In return, the management put on a magnificent show, hiring internationally celebrated performers at fees that could rise to 500 guineas a night for a singer of the calibre of Christine Nilsson.

But it was not only for the singing that one attended the opera. Pascoe records:

> To go to the opera, to see and hear the great singers of the day, and listen to the finest works of the world's composers, admirably rendered by an exceptionally fine orchestra, conducted by someone of first-rate ability, are unquestionably inducements with a good many; but they are not the sole inducements the Royal Opera House, Covent Garden, offers in the full of the London Season.
>
> It is then the greatest rendezvous of Fashionable Society, in which Royalty, the aristocracy, the leaders in every walk of life, and the wealthy have their place; in which the dress of the ladies, no less than their beauty, are points of great attractiveness; and in which displays of every kind, magnificent jewels, beautiful bouquets, variety of colour, and the vastness and brilliance of the house itself, are to be considered in the programme of the evening's entertainment. It is true one pays handsomely for enjoying it—but then look what you get for your money!

The same sentiments are echoed in this longer account by the cynical but nonetheless starry-eyed author of *The Night Side of London*:

> The opening night of the Opera Season at Covent Garden is always one of the chief events of the Season—to many it is *the* event. There is plenty of music of all kinds to be heard in London all the year round, but the Opera at Covent Garden is its highest expression. The Opera House itself is not an impressive building, comparing none too favourably with the opera-houses of Paris, of Vienna, or even New York. But on the opening night of the Season, or on a night when a great singer is to appear, there is no more brilliant sight to be seen in any land than the interior of Covent Garden.

The Party That Lasted 100 Days

Long before the hour announced for the curtain to be raised, carriages in a row half a mile in length stand, or slowly crawl towards the door under the portico, their movements carefully guarded and regulated by the police. Some minutes before the curtain goes up the auditorium is packed with as many great, distinguished or rich people as it can hold. It is a wonderful society gathering. Here is Everybody that is Anybody—*tout le monde et sa femme*. And amongst them it is just possible there are some genuine lovers of music.

You are so much taken up with looking about you at the brilliant ensemble that you pay no heed at first to the orchestra tuning up. But you do notice the conductor enter and, baton in hand, bow to the audience. Presently the curtain is raised, and discloses the company. The prima donna comes a little step forward—everyone rises while she sings the first verse of the National Anthem. Then, everybody, having engaged in this exercise, sits down, his sentiment of loyalty gratified. In a minute or two more the opera begins—it is rarely a new opera—the old favourites are preferred, always with the exception of Wagnerian opera, which has come to stay.

Below
Christine Nilsson at the Albert Hall.
Graphic, *1888*

Above
Advertisement from Herbert's London Guide, *1883*

Right *After the opera.*
Graphic, *1870*

The social side of the thing is to be seen in visits paid from box to box in the intervals, and the smoking foyer is a centre where men meet and compare notes, though it is tolerably certain the notes will not be concerned so much with the music as with the people who are present. 'Isn't Lady So-and-So looking remarkably well tonight? Wonder how she does it—She's fifty if she's a day! Wonderful! And look at little Laura! She's another wonder. Did you see *he* was in the box? Well, if her husband can stand it, it's all right, I suppose.' And so on and so on.

Somewhere around midnight the opera comes to an end. Perhaps you go home, or perhaps you go to supper at somebody else's, for there are some superb supper-parties given after the opera's over. Or you may go to one of the clubs, where you will have something to eat, and exchange more gossip about your neighbours.

Chapter 9
DAYS AT THE RACES

Bearing in mind Society's country origins, we need not be surprised that its favourite amusements were country sports. Even after its members had voluntarily incarcerated themselves in Town for the urban delights of the Season, there is little doubt that the occasions which excited their greatest enthusiasm were Ascot and Henley, with other sporting occasions hardly less prominent on the social calendar.

However, Society would not have been Society if it had not touched these events with its golden wand and invested them with all the paraphernalia of ceremonial with which it conducted the rest of its doings. Ascot became no longer merely a horse race, Henley no longer merely a boat race. Some of the less important events — the horse races at Sandown and Kempton Park for example — remained primarily occasions on which horses were made to run against one another while men and sometimes ladies wagered money on the result. But three of the race meetings developed over the years into more than that — the Derby in early June, Ascot later in the same month, and Goodwood at the end of July.

THE DERBY

The Derby is just one of the many races run at Epsom during the June meeting, but this $2\frac{1}{2}$-minute event had long held a special place in the public's favour, and was the chief focus of the horse-racing year. People swarmed to Epsom who never attended any other race meeting; people bet on the Derby who never laid money on any other event.

As far as Society was concerned, the Derby was rather *too* popular. Nobody could even begin to pretend that there was anything exclusive about it. Derby Day was patently the greatest popular festival of the year, and belonged to everyone, to the public at large rather than to any specific section of it. Which meant, statistically, that it was largely the working man's affair, as Richard Harding Davis noted:

Of course there were other classes there, the idle rich and royalties, but they were not on the scene at all. They formed a cluster of black hats in a corner of a grandstand that rose

Opposite
The Derby.
ILN, *1871,*
and London
Society, *1863*

as high as the Equitable Building—a wall of human beings with faces for bricks. The real Derby crowd was that which stretched about this sheer wall upon Epsom Downs over miles and miles of dusty turf.

No commentator on the English social scene would dare to leave out Derby Day; no foreign visitor would consider he had collected a representative set of impressions of the British character if he had not seen the Briton on Epsom Downs. Pascoe's description is as eloquent as any:

Race-meetings near London draw together as choice a collection of blackguards and vagabonds of every degree as anywhere congregate. And these bring in their train a motley herd of camp-followers, sellers of pig's feet, shell-fish, 'snacks', and what-not, who profit by the holiday—the most honest workers among the lot. On the fringe of the crowd the stranger will notice some splendid 'swells' and others less splendid, several 'pals' and poor little tight-trousered clerks, and 'orty Mr Jeames de la Pluche, and 'is friend 'Sir 'Arry' (who've got off from the 'ouse for an hour or so), and a very great number of boys and men carrying sporting journals and scraps of paper scanning the betting. Not a twentieth part of them know anything about a horse, but you are to believe they do. The journey down they will as glibly discourse to you anent the particular qualities of 'the Duke's' and 'Baron's' lots as if they had been bred in the trainer's stables. Any stranger who has taken part in this great gathering of Englishmen need not trouble to journey to another race-course; if he has seen the 'Derby' run, the remembrance of that scene will last a lifetime. To strict amateurs of the Turf, the Epsom meeting is a mere national junketing; for the million, it embodies all that need be wanted to make a holiday. All England turns out and joins in the frolic, even though the great majority of the holiday-makers care less for the great event of the day than if it had been a race of donkeys jockeyed by wooden-legged naval pensioners.

It is not surprising that in earlier decades Society had considered the Derby beneath it; but as even the élite grew more broad-minded, things changed. Montagu Williams observed:

Ladies never, or very seldom, went to the Derby forty years ago. They were content with gracing the Epsom gradients on the 'ladies day' when the Oaks was run. Things are very different now. The boxes and stands are crowded with ladies. Racing has become almost as great an amusement for fashionable women as for fashionable men, and though the former do not wager in such high figures as the latter, they are pretty universally imbued with the spirit of gambling. Thus it comes about that London is pretty well filled by the week in which the carnival of the English turf takes place.

ASCOT

Ascot was quite another matter. Ascot Week was the half-way point of the London Season, and for many its highest point. As a race meeting, it was the one which

Days At The Races

provided the best sport of the year: it offered the largest sums in prize money. But it was even more as a social event that Ascot claimed pre-eminence. 'You have not "done" London—fashionable London—until you have trod the Lawn at Ascot,' Pascoe declared. To attend on at least one day, Gold Cup day, was a virtual obligation on everyone who was anyone in Society. Here they gathered, usually by coach, in a line stretching for over a quarter of a mile and three or four vehicles deep, Society's most dazzling picnic.

As for the picnic 'eats', they were in keeping with the occasion. Here is one writer's suggestion for the refreshments at an Ascot Party, which would of course be carried to the meeting in hampers and consumed on the coach, served by the grooms in conditions of considerable inconvenience:

AN ASCOT PARTY

Salade de Homard
Saumon, Sauce Raifort glacé
Boeuf rôti
Pâté de Poularde et Pigeon
Poulets rôtis
Langues de Boeuf
Asperges Marinés
Côtelettes à la Connaught

Sandwiches variés

Méringues à la Crême
Bouchées Pralinées
Eclairs au chocolat

GLACES
Crême de Fraises
Eau de Limon

Thé et Café

Gâteaux et Biscuits

The writer makes no mention of the other drinks available, but we need not suppose that the choice was limited to lemonade, tea or coffee. Champagne corks must have made quite a high proportion of the litter that strewed the ground after the carriages and their occupants had departed.

Once again, the best accounts of the event are those seen through foreign eyes:

Ascot Heath is a sloping ridge of moorland some thirty miles from London, the crest of which looks away across the Windsor woods to the plains of Bucks and Middlesex. Ascot races take place at the very high tide of the Season. They are the Eden of débutantes and

→114

Days At The Races

Scenes from Ascot: (above) *arrival of the
Prince and Princess of Wales.* Graphic, *1882*

Below *The royal enclosure.* Graphic, *1895*

Inside the royal enclosure. Graphic, *1889*

Opposite *The drive through Windsor Park.* ILN, *1871*

the milliners' harvest. Various modes of enjoying the delights of Ascot are in vogue. Some persons take one of the numerous villa residences with which the neighbourhood abounds, and many of which pay their year's rent by letting for this one week. Others drive down daily from London on a friend's coach. Then there is the large class who toil down by train, the women in dust coats and veils, and the men in light paletots.

A greater show of good looks and good clothes combined is hardly to be found at any other butterflies' feast in the world. For most women go to Ascot mainly to show their gowns, which have been the subject of much anxious thought, and are an interesting index to the character of their wearers. Any new or striking development in this line displayed at Ascot may in a week be flaring in the remotest provinces. Everyone who can extract a ticket from the Master of the Buckhounds goes to the royal enclosure; those who cannot, take boxes, or view the races from the 'drags'. To a large portion of the spectators the races are almost as great a bore as the cricket at the Eton and Harrow match. There are, however, exceptions, even among the fair sex, some of whom find it pays to be lovers of horseflesh.

(*Harpers*, 1886)

One finds the Cup Day of Royal Ascot a somewhat tame affair after the rowdy good nature and vast extent of the Derby. It is neither the one thing nor the other. There is rather too much dust and too frequent intrusions of horses upon the scene to make it a successful garden party, and there are too many women to make it a thoroughly sporting race meeting. There seem to be at least four women to every man.

The crowd that makes the Derby what it is, is only present at Ascot on sufferance. The smart people, to whom Ascot primarily and solely belongs, have all the best places and the best time; but even the best time does not seem to be a very good time. They all appear to be afraid of mussing their frocks which, when they have so many, seems rather mean-spirited.

There is a track at Ascot over which horses run at great speed at irregular intervals, but nobody takes them seriously. One is either back in the Royal Enclosure taking tea, or behind the grandstand on the Lawn, quite out of sight of the track, or lunching on the long line of coaches facing it, or in the club and regimental tents back of these where, for all one can see of it, the race might be coming off in Piccadilly.

Every well-known regiment has its own luncheon tent, and many of the London clubs also, and the pretty women, and the big narrow-waisted young men, all of whom look and walk and dress alike—even to the yellow leather field-glass over the right shoulder, which never comes out of its case—pass from tent to tent, and from coach to coach, and from the Enclosure to the grandstand throughout the whole of the day, seeking acquaintances and luncheon, and tasting horrible claret-cup and warm champagne.

The Ascot races were under the especial charge last year of the Earl of Coventry, who, as Master of the Queen's Buckhounds, had, among other duties, that of refusing the applications of five thousand people for a place in the Enclosure. This in itself must be something of a responsibility, although it is likely that after one has refused three thousand, the other two thousand would not weigh on one's mind.

To the American there must always be something delightful in the idea of the Enclosure —but the reality is a trifle disappointing. He has, of course, outgrown the idea that royalties look differently from other people, but such an aggregation of social celebrities penned up, as it were, and on view to such an immense mob, seems to promise something less conventional. But it is interesting to hear the present bearer of a very great name fuss

Goodwood:
Above right
A general view.
Graphic, *1887*

Below right
The hill in the park. Graphic, *1885*

and fret because there are two and not three lumps in his tea, and to find that the very much made-up lady is *the* professional beauty, and *not* the young and very beautiful one who is laughing so heartily at a song of a coloured comedian on the other side of the rail, and that she in turn was once a clergyman's daughter and is now a Personage indeed, and 'walks in' before all the other great ladies and professional beauties and the young girl friends of her own age with whom she once used to play tennis and do parish work.

It is also curious to consider that the young man who is sitting down while three women are standing and talking to him is a manufacturer's son who is worth ten million pounds sterling. It is also interesting to hear the policemen tell the crowd outside the fence that they must not even 'touch the railing'. I really could not see what harm it would have done had they happened to touch the railing itself, especially when it was the fault of those behind who were so keen to see. And it is only fair to say that the lions behaved admirably, and were quite unconscious of the presence of so many awe-stricken spectators. That is all that saved it from being ridiculous on both sides of the barrier.

(Richard Harding Davis, *Harpers*, 1893)

GOODWOOD

Below *The Ladies' Lawn.* ILN, *1864*

Goodwood is Ascot over again, with fewer 'citizens' and 'alarms and excursions' of the London betting gang. There are generally the same horses, the same jockeys, the same sets of 'swells', the same smart frocks and bonnets, the same grand array of delicacies and drinks.

(Pascoe, *London of Today*)

Of the three great horse-racing events, Goodwood was the most exclusive so far as Society was concerned—partly because it was the farthest from London, offering less temptation to the average Londoner to take a day out. It was held in one of the prettiest race-grounds in England, amid charming scenery, close to the country seat of the Duke of Richmond—and this, too, helped to give it a more aristocratic character. From the sporting point of view it was not so important as either Epsom or Ascot. The Prince of Wales aptly said of it, that it was 'a garden party with racing tacked on'.

Perhaps the greatest significance of Goodwood was that it marked the end of the Season. It was the last major event, and was in part a climax, in part a farewell. Not that it was a farewell for long—the same people who had been meeting and mingling at receptions and dances for the past three months, who were meeting one another today at Goodwood, would all be meeting again soon enough at Cowes, or on the Scottish grouse-moors, or in one another's country homes.

Chapter 10
SPORTING OCCASIONS

Whether or not the English invented sport, they have always behaved as if they did, and in the latter half of the nineteenth century they surpassed themselves in their devotion to every kind of sporting activity. There were fluctuations in fashion: such amusing pastimes as bear-baiting and cock-fighting were chiefly confined to the north of England, while prize-fighting, formerly patronised by aristocrats like Lord Byron, had lost status and, though as popular as ever, was followed almost entirely by the working classes. Horse-racing, as we have already seen, was as much the 'Sport of Kings' as ever, and hunting in its various forms continued to be the prerogative of those who owned the land on which the hunting took place, and so was largely an upper-class amusement.

If education at an English public school taught a boy nothing else, it equipped him to play his part in the sporting field. The young men of Society, however backward they might be in the ballroom, were ready to work hard at other forms of play. The ladies had to go along with this, if they wished to win the young men's favour; and so they would go out to Hurlingham to watch the men play polo, and perhaps even join them in a match of tennis. Other pastimes in which young ladies could work off their surplus energy—and at the same time display their figures to advantage—were archery and croquet, both of which could be indulged in at the various clubs in the suburbs.

However, only a very few sporting events attained the status of Society functions. One of the few was the annual cricket match between the schoolboys of Eton and those of Harrow, which took place at Lord's cricket ground at Marylebone during the second week of July. Since a very high proportion of the young men of Society had been educated at one or other of these establishments, it was not surprising that many members of Society might take an interest. It started with parents and old boys going to Lord's to watch the game and taking their own refreshments with them; gradually the event grew into a great Society picnic, more of a social event than a sporting fixture—Pascoe in 1902 wrote that 'the Eton and Harrow match is an affair of bonnets, dresses, frock-coats, lobster-salads and champagne—a very "swell" picnic, in fact'.

Wherever the space round the ground is unoccupied by stands, there are rows of carriages

Above left *Archery for ladies at the Royal
Toxophilite Society's grounds, Regent's Park.*
Graphic, *1870*

Above right *Croquet.* Graphic, *1870*

Above *Eton* v. *Harrow at Lord's.* Graphic, *1872*

three or four deep. They are sent up the day before to places that have been allotted them, and the horses taken out. From four-fifths of these carriages nothing of the game is visible—nor is there any reason why there should be, for only about a fifth of the spectators care for the cricket. Most of the vehicles serve as depots for large cold luncheons, which are administered to the friends of the owner by unfortunate servants, who carve chickens and uncork champagne bottles on all fours between the wheels.

Where possible, the meal is made still more elaborate by being served on a temporary table—and in all the vacant corners members of the aristocracy and the Stock Exchange may be seen eating and drinking in public. Unsatisfied friends keep dropping in, and the popping of corks goes on till late in the day, when the flushed revellers begin on tea and fruit. On the whole, the exhibition is not a satisfactory one, having a tendency to grossness, and preventing people from seeing the cricket who wish to do so.

(*Harpers*, 1886)

The ever-helpful 'Madge' of *Truth* was ready with practical suggestions as to the refreshments:

Saumon à la Zingari
Salade de Homard

The Party That Lasted 100 Days

Chaudfroids de Cailles à la Royale
Poulets rôtis aux Cresson
Galantines de Volaille
Jambon de York

SANDWICHES
Aux Cresson
de Langues
Croûtes de Foies Gras

Glaces   Fruits

COACHING MEETS

Below and
opposite *The
Four-in-Hand
Club in Hyde
Park.*
Graphic,
1892 and 1887

Society people were 'horsey' people. The railway was too democratic an institution, even with its coaches carefully apportioned to the various social classes—a duke who ventured to travel by train might find himself sharing a compartment with anyone who chose to pay the price of a first-class ticket. So, whenever possible, Society used horse-drawn transport, and in its leisure played at reviving the great age of the stage-coach, now largely vanished from the roads of England for half a century.

Coaching became a cult in the latter decades of the nineteenth century comparable with that of the veteran motor car today. The two best-known coaching clubs were the Four-in-Hand Club and the Coaching Club, which were able to muster in 1902 a total of 27 and 34 coaches respectively. The Coaching Club traditionally held its opening meeting in Hyde Park on the Wednesday before Derby Day, while the

Four-in-Hand followed suit a week later.

It was an expensive amusement. The coach itself would cost about £500, not to mention repairs and upkeep; the four horses would cost another £1000 at the very least. Two grooms were carried, each of whom would need to be paid £80 to £100 a year, plus his keep and accommodation; the grooms' uniforms of breeches, top-boots and coats would be an additional item. Pascoe comments with unusual acidity:

> When all are mustered, the coaches start (with a number of 'swells' seated outside) with becoming solemnity, and oftentimes no little difficulty, and make the tour of Hyde Park, some perhaps going as far as Hurlingham or the Crystal Palace to lunch. One would have thought that this absurd and useless 'ceremony' could have little interest save for the distinguished members of the clubs and their friends. Yet year after year it attracts thousands of spectators, who are massed in the vicinity of the Powder Magazine, Hyde Park, and at other points along the line of route.

HENLEY REGATTA

After Ascot, the most important out-of-town event in the social calendar was unquestionably Henley; like Ascot, it had come to acquire a symbolic status out of all proportion—and largely unrelated—to its sporting significance. There were, after all, many other regattas; there were other regattas on the Thames. But Henley-on-Thames offered a combination of a reasonable proximity to London with a convenient date in the calendar, with the result that Society 'adopted' it and marked

Two views of Henley. Graphic, *1891 and* ILN, *1893*

it for its own. So from a local rural festival the Henley Regatta grew to the proportions of a national holiday; for three days in July the quiet little Thames-side town was invaded by Society, and by Society's hangers-on.

Our percipient American observer, Richard Harding Davis, once again gives us a characteristically colourful description:

What impresses you most about Henley is the way in which everyone contributes to make it what it is. It is not divided into those who are looked at and those who look on. Everyone helps, from the young man in the blue coat and the red ribbon of the Leander Club who lounges on the house-boat, to the perspiring waterman, with his brass shield and red coat, who ferries you from one bank to the other. The chance spectator gives just as much to the scene as does the winner of the Diamond Sculls. Everyone and every boat load is part of a great panorama of colour and movement, some giving more than others. Letty Lind, of the Gaiety Theatre, for instance, under her lace parasol in the Gaiety enclosure, is more pleasing to look at than the stout gentleman who is bumping everything within reach of his punt, and who is kept busy begging pardons from one end of the course to the other; but even he makes you smile lazily, and so contributes to the whole.

The rules which govern the Henley week are as strictly in force as those which govern the Bank of England. A governing committee, or board of trustees, or some such important body, sit in conclave long before Henley week, and receive applications from clubs for places along the bank, and from families for portions of the lawns, and from the owners of house-boats for positions on the course. And so when you come down from Town in your flannels, prepared to be pleased and to enjoy yourself, you find the scene set, and the ushers in their places, and your seat reserved for you. That is the great thing about England—its law and order, which keeps the hired carriages out of the Row, which arrests you for throwing an envelope out of a hansom-cab, and which controls the position of your canoe at Henley.

The racing is a very small part of Henley. It must necessarily be so when two boats only can row at the same time, and when the advantage of position means an advantage of two lengths to the crew which can pull under the shelter of the house-boats. An arrangement so absurd as that cannot be considered as coming under the head of serious sport. Henley is a great water-picnic, not a sporting event; it is the out-of-door life, the sight of the thousands of boats and thousands of people in white and colours, all on pleasure bent, and the green trees, and beautiful flowers on the houseboats, and the coloured lanterns at night and the fireworks, which make Henley an institution.

You enter into the spirit of Henley when you get your ticket in Town, and find hundreds of young men and maidens crowding the platform, and dressed as no one would dare to dress in New York city—in the most barbarous blazers and brilliant boating suits. America is a fine free country in many ways, but England is much more free in one, and allows her subjects or the strangers within her gates to dress as they please, and where they please.

From the big stone bridge to a point a mile below, the house-boats stretch along one bank, and green grass and high trees line the other, and on the river between are processions and processions of boats, so close that the owners touch with their hands; they move along in blocks, or pull out of the crush by stealing a tow from the boat just ahead. A skilful and agile athlete could cross the river dry-shod at places by stepping from one boat to another. The boats and their crews disappear and reappear like a shuttle in a loom, moving slowly in and out, or shooting ahead if they are small enough, and you catch a glimpse of a pretty face or a more than striking costume only to lose it again as another boat slips in the way like the slide in a stereopticon.

Whether you look down upon it from a houseboat or are in the midst of it in a canoe, the effect is more brilliant and the changes more bewildering than are the advancing and retreating lines of any great ballet you have ever seen. And at night, even when you try to sleep, you still see the colours and the shining sunlight flashing on the polished woodwork, and the boats as they move in and out and swallow each other up.

The setting of the scene is very good. Nature has been the landscape-gardener of one bank with trees and gradually rising hills, and man has made the other brilliant with a long row of houseboats. A houseboat can be a very modest and barnlike affair, or it can suggest a bower of fresh flowers and a floating Chinese pagoda combined. Those at Henley are of this latter kind. Some of them were pink and white, with rows of pink carnations, or white and gold, with hanging vines of green, or brilliantly blue, with solid banks of red geraniums. Some of them were hidden entirely by long wooden boxes of growing flowers, which overflowed and hung down in masses of colour to the water's edge, and all had gorgeously striped awnings and Chinese umbrellas and soft Persian rugs everywhere, and silk flags of the owners' own design flapping overhead. It is only a step along the gang-plank to the lawn, and so on down the line to the next open space, where some club has a bit of lawn reserved for it, and has erected a marquee, and brilliant standards proclaiming its name, and guiding the thirsty and hungry member to its luncheon table.

There are possibly more profitable ways of employing one's time and more intellectual amusements, but you are very near to content when you fall back in a wicker chair on the

A picnic at Henley. ILN, *1888*

top of one of these water-houses, and feel the breeze lifting the awning overhead, and hear the trees scraping it with their leaves—and were it not for the necessity of getting up to watch two crews of young men pulling violently past at an unusual speed, the race week at Henley would be quite ideal.

As for the refreshments provided, they surpass any of the menus quoted in this book both in their quantity and in their quality:

Xeres Sec	Bonne Bouche de Crevettes
	Mousse de Foies Gras
	Tomâtes Marinades
Haut Sauterne	Saumon, Sauce Verte
	Homard à la Patti
	Salade
	Cailles en Caisses
	Poulets rôtis aux Cresson
	Langue de Boeuf
Pommery Greno, 1889	Ponche à la Romaine
Magnums Bollinger, 1884	Targe d'Agneau
	Pois à la Marinés
	Sirloin de Boeuf
	Pâtisseries Genoises
Benedictine, Crême de Cacao	Glaces Variées
Liqueur Brandy, 1875	Café Froid
Clos de Vougeot, 1888	Gâteaux Variés
Château Lafitte, 1877	Biscuits Assortis
	Bread and butter
Gallinari	Fruits
Port (Crofts) 1863	
	Thé et Café (chaud)

That little repast was scheduled for 1 p.m., and you could hardly hope to get through it in less than a couple of hours. Yet at 4 p.m. you were expected to toy with tea—admittedly, a very light one:

Strawberry Cream Ice
Lemon Water Ice
Iced Coffee
Tea
Bread and Butter
Cakes and Biscuits

Henley after dark. Graphic, 1892

Aboard a house-boat. Graphic, *1898*

(Incidentally, there is no doubt something significant in the fact that at tea-time the preparer of these menus lapses into English; no doubt it was regarded as a fair tribute to the race which had given the world '*le five o'clock*'.)

After tea, you were permitted a reasonable break during which you would be well advised to exert yourself in the hope of working up an appetite for supper, which, though light enough by the standards of the day, was still a substantial meal by most accounts:

> Poulets à la Béchamel
> Boeuf épicé
> Salades Françaises
> Gelées aux Fruits
> Petits Fours
> Fraises et Crême

No drink is specified, but we may assume the ubiquitous champagne, whose corks must have been seen drifting down the river back to Town in generous profusion during that busy sporting week.

130

Chapter 11
PRESENTED AT COURT

What is the real purpose in going to Court? Is it, in truth, in order that you may pay your respects to Royalty? Nonsense; in nine cases out of ten it is in order to see and be seen, to have your name noted by *The Times* or *Morning Post*, to appear more magnificently attired than someone else, to have your dress very fully described in the ladies' journals, to be photographed in that dress at midnight in Bond Street, and generally for the sake of having it known that you have been at Court.

(Pascoe, *London of Today*, 1903)

It would be almost impossible not to allow one's prejudices for or against the Monarchy to colour an account of that crowning experience in a débutante's life, Presentation at Court. Accounts of the affair range from dewy-eyed awe to sneering contempt: in the face of such a divergence of response, I have tried to chronicle the sequence of events as objectively as possible. To add colour to the account, comments are included from a gushing but most informative description which Mary Howarth contributed to the *Pall Mall* Magazine in 1902. All the quotations are from this source unless otherwise attributed.

First, who was entitled to be presented to the Monarch? The qualifications were identical with those for attendance at Her Majesty's Drawing Rooms, for, once having been presented to the Queen, a lady was expected to attend one Drawing Room a year, and would be invited to one State Ball each season.

The persons entitled to attend Her Majesty's Drawing Rooms are the wives and daughters of the members of the aristocracy, the country gentry and town gentry, the wives and daughters of the members of the legal, military, naval, clerical, medical and other professions, the wives and daughters of merchants, bankers, and members of the Stock Exchange, and persons engaged in commerce on a large scale. Although the word gentry is thus elastic, and although persons coming within the category might be fairly entitled to the privilege of attending Drawing Rooms, yet it is well understood that birth, wealth, associations and position give a *raison d'être* for such privileges.

(*Manners and Rules of Good Society*)

If a lady wanted to be presented, she had first to find someone to present her. This had to be someone who had herself been presented, and who must be married. The

On the way to a Drawing Room at Buckingham Palace. ILN. *1870*

ceremony took place at one of the four annual Drawing Rooms, which Victoria held at Buckingham Palace in the 1890s, though previously she had held them at St James's Palace. In view of her age, Victoria held her Drawing Rooms in the afternoon; she usually attended in person for the first hour or so, and then retired leaving her daughter-in-law, Princess Alexandra, to do the honours instead. On the afternoon on which Lily Langtry was presented, however, Victoria stayed on until that lady appeared, so curious was she to see the phenomenon that all London was talking about.

The initial application was made to the Lord Chamberlain for two cards; on these she stated who she was, whom she was related to, and who was going to present her. The lady who proposed to present her had to countersign one of the cards, which were then returned to the Lord Chamberlain so that he could obtain the Queen's approval.

If the Lord Chamberlain gave her the go-ahead at this stage, naming the day, she would then have to apply for two more cards, which she filled in with the appropriate information to hand in, one as she arrived at the Palace and the other just before the moment of Presentation.

The ceremony required quite a lot of preparation. Dress, in particular, was of vital importance. Not only must it be as striking as the dressmaker's skill could make it, to outshine her friends, but it must also conform to the strict requirements of the Court:

> The lady courtier must appear in full evening toilette, the corsage cut low to outline the shoulders, the sleeves extremely short. She must wear a Court train of three and a half to four yards long, white gloves, a white veil hanging from three plumes, which must be white if she is not in mourning, black if she is.

Ladies of delicate health could obtain permission to wear a half-high corsage and elbow sleeves, so long as their application to the Lord Chamberlain was accompanied by a doctor's certificate. Otherwise, each lady had to do what she could within the limitations laid down. Her bodice and petticoat were generally of matching silk, and her train, which could be from the waist or shoulders, was generally of velvet or satin, trimmed with lace. She wore lace lappets and as much in the way of precious stones as she could muster, and she carried a fan.

The Drawing Room took place generally at 2 or 3 p.m.; the previous hours were spent in anguished preparation. Lady's maids and hairdressers would have been busy all day: some nervous ladies even had their hair done the previous day. Well ahead of the appointed time, the applicant set off for the Palace in her coach—a state car-riage, if her family owned or could borrow one. For hours the carriages waited in line along the Mall, affording amusement to the crowds of unprivileged persons who congregated round the carriages, passing remarks and making invidious but generally admiring comparisons.

> The courtiers had to bear hours of unceasing fatigue that day—hours in their carriages on their slow way to the Palace, hours in the Palace itself, hours later before they at length reached their homes. But for the sake of the supreme second during which they and their Queen or future Queen were as friend and friend, face to face, double and treble the exertion would have been endured with pleasure . . .

When eventually the courtier's carriage deposited her at the Palace, she went in, leaving her wraps in the cloak room and prosaically receiving a numbered ticket in exchange. She crossed the Great Hall, and ascended the Grand Staircase to the Corridor. Here she was shown into one of the ante-chambers, through a succession of which she had to pass, one of a group of thirty or so admitted at a time by Gentlemen-at-Arms manning gilt barriers.

> There are most comfortable settee benches en route, little use of which is made as a rule, because everyone wants to arrive in the Royal presence unruffled, and besides, there is a very general tendency to press forward as fast as possible. Eager, insistent members of the

The Party That Lasted 100 Days

At the foot of the stairs. Graphic, *1895*

Below
Preparing to enter the Throne Room. 1898

throng push and struggle to make a way for themselves with unbecoming vigour, and debutantes distressful are parted from chaperons indignant . . .

Those privileged to possess the entrée—that is, those who were attached to the Court in some way, or members of diplomatic circles—took precedence. Apart from this, it was a matter of first come, first served, and a fair amount of pushing and shoving took place—partly because the earlier you were in the queue, the greater your chance of being presented to Victoria herself instead of having to settle for Alexandra, and partly because, the ordeal of presentation over, you could then relax, forget about keeping your dress immaculate, and start to enjoy the affair.

Gradually the débutante approached the Presence Chamber:

Delicious, though fraught with such racking anxieties, are the tremors that assail the debutante before her presentation. To her imagination the ordeal before her looms large and terrible. It is as if she were called upon to face her Sovereign, chief actress in an unrehearsed scene, the whole success of which depends upon herself. Yet she may absolutely trust to the exquisite and ceremonious care which will attend her every footstep on the way from the Palace door to their Majesties' presence; and provided she literally obeys every injunction she receives, and keeps close to her chaperon, she cannot possibly err.

At the door of the Picture Gallery her train, which up till now she had been carrying on her arm, was taken by two of the Gentlemen-at-Arms and spread out by them on the floor with their wands. She then removed her right glove and, with her train down, crossed the Gallery to the door of the Presence Chamber. Here she presented her second card, which was passed from hand to hand by Court servants until it was given to the Lord Chamberlain himself, who read it out aloud as the débutante presented herself.

If the débutante was a peeress or a peer's daughter, Victoria would kiss her on the cheek or forehead, which meant that she had to get herself into a suitable position to be kissed by the very short Queen, while maintaining her stance and managing her train. If she was not a peeress or peer's daughter, she had to kiss the Queen's hand, which she did by placing her own hand beneath the Queen's, while curtseying. No doubt the manoeuvre had been well practised at home beforehand.

If it was to Princess Alexandra that the débutante was being presented, there would be no kissing of hands or cheeks: instead, she would simply curtsey. She would then curtsey to any other member of the Royal Family who happened to be around—which could very well be a matter of making half-a-dozen separate obeisances, stepping backwards all the time—for she must never turn her back upon her Sovereign—and at the same time managing her train as best she could.

Finally she reached the exit door and emerged, safe at last from the possibility of calamity. Her train was picked up and restored to her arm, and she was free to pass

→ 138

Presented to Her Majesty. Graphic, *1893*   Opposite *The Royal Hand.* Graphic, *1875*

through to the supper room on those occasions when refreshments were served (which during Victoria's reign were not very often: Edward and Alexandra were more thoughtful).

The next move was generally to the photographer's, so that the débutante could be immortalised in the full splendour of her Court dress. During Edward's reign, when the Drawing Rooms were held at night, the Bond Street photographers would stay open till three in the morning, taking portrait after portrait of proud young ladies, who would then proceed to a celebratory party, known as a 'peacock' or 'train' tea, given in honour of the occasion. In Victoria's day, when the débutante emerged in daylight, it was a custom for many to drive in Hyde Park, 'where the congregated crowds feasted their eyes upon the flower of the nation's beauty and chivalry in all their splendid attire'.

And then it was all over; the seal had been set on the girl's début, she had received the greatest honour she was ever likely to receive. But the etiquette books sound a final warning note:

Should any person be presented whose antecedents or present position render her socially unqualified to be presented, the Lord Chamberlain on becoming aware of the fact would at once cancel the presentation, and officially announce it in the *Gazette*, and the person making such presentation would be expected to tender an apology.

At the photographer's.
Graphic, *1895*

Chapter 12
SOMEONE HAS TO DO THE WORK

Society was frequently attacked for its extravagant ways, even in an age which was largely committed to the view that God created man either high or lowly and ordered his estate to match. For the vast majority, the London Season was a matter of complete indifference; for the minority who participated in it, it was one of great importance; for another minority, it was a social evil, an offence against justice and democracy.

Such attacks did not, as might have been expected, come chiefly from the non-conformist critics whose puritan ethics drove them to condemn smoking, drinking, gambling and fornication: this may have been because reformist societies were more concerned to have the names of the leaders of society on their lists of patrons. Criticism was political rather than religious: it was the socialist editor Robert Blatchford who converted the Countess of Warwick to socialism in the course of a single afternoon, when she had rushed indignantly round to his office to upbraid him for censuring in his journal the extravagance of one of her more spectacular entertainments.

The argument generally put forward by Society in its own justification, and doubtless employed on that occasion by the furious Countess, was that Society provided valuable employment for the less privileged sections of the population. Here is that argument, as expressed in all seriousness by Lady Dorothy Neville, one of the most prominent social arbiters of the 1890s:

> From time to time London Society is attacked for its luxurious ways and for spending too much money on its pleasures. As a matter of fact, the success of the London Season is of immense importance to a number of poor people whose life does not, at first sight, seem connected with it. A bad Season is a calamity to be deplored.
>
> If a diminution in social gaieties merely affected the well-to-do and the frivolous, there might be some reason for deploring the sums spent on entertainment; but a far wider circle of individuals than is generally supposed suffer from a bad Season, for the money expended in the West End during the summer months distributes itself far and wide amongst the poorer classes of the town, and a dull Season, therefore, entails much disappointment and even distress. That which affects Belgravia is unfortunately sure to react upon Whitechapel. For this reason those whose circumstances permit them to entertain should do so, even at some sacrifice to themselves, in order to benefit their

EMBARRASSING.   1885.

(*Mrs. Colonel Smythe (of the Poonah Hussars) explains in fluent Hindostanee to her Sister, Mrs. Major Browne (ditto), that the same article can be got at the Army and Navy Stores for two-thirds of the money.*)

Draper. "AHEM—I BEG PARDON, LADIES, BUT I THINK IT ONLY FAIR TO ACQUAINT YOU THAT I UNDERSTAND THE FRENCH LANGUAGE!"

humbler and more dependent neighbours. Notwithstanding the plausible theories of political economists, experience proves that thousands of meritorious and industrious people procure an honest livelihood through ministering directly or indirectly to pleasure and amusement.

The vast increase of luxury which has taken place during the last twenty years has without doubt helped to save large numbers of people from poverty, besides affording employment to hundreds, even thousands, of girls, milliners and the like, who have largely profited by the enormously increased attention bestowed upon female dress.

It would be wrong to claim that there is no logic at all in this line of argument; but, as Robert Blatchford pointed out to the Countess of Warwick, it rests upon a fallacy—like the argument that would defend wars because of the employment provided by armament manufacture. Labour expended on extravagance is labour wasted. Even though in the short term those workers who have committed themselves to living off Society's extravagance do indeed derive a living by so doing, they ally themselves with a system of injustice and have no right to complain if the system lets them down.

However, for good or ill, Lady Dorothy was undoubtedly correct when she claimed that the London Season was of great commercial importance. We have only to consider the vast army of men and women, not members of Society, whose skills and patience were required to make the Season possible—regiments of servants, shopkeepers, caterers and entertainers, whose number far and away exceeded that of the favoured few who enjoyed the more immediate benefits.

ENTERTAINERS

While entertainers were not wholly dependent on Society, the Season undoubtedly stimulated their trade. Would there have been an opera season without *the* Season? Would those prima donnas have been brought over from Milan and Vienna at £500 a performance? Would London have been able to maintain quite so many theatres and concert halls?

The Season employed a horde of professional musicians—pianists and ensembles who provided the music for dances, several of them every night, from 11 p.m. till three or four in the morning. The newspapers had columns of advertisements like these:

IL QUINTETTO NAPOLITANO, Mandolinists, Guitarists and Vocalists, for

Advertisement, 1895

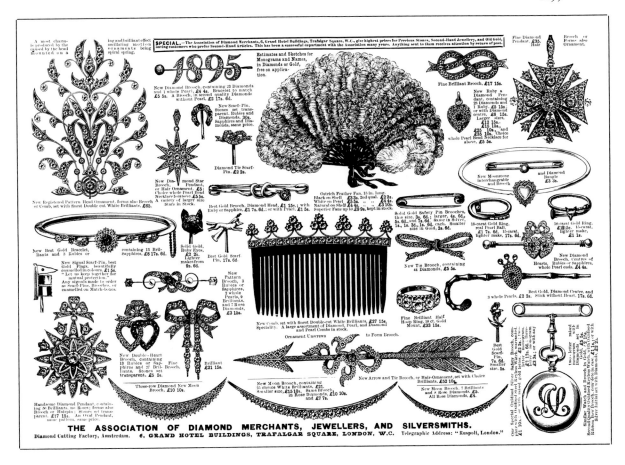

receptions and garden parties, the most complete and representative company that have ever visited England. Sole agents, Lacon & Ollier.

MITCHELL'S BLUE HUNGARIAN BAND has arrived in London for the Season and arrangements have been made whereby it may be engaged as a Band of either twelve, nine or six performers. Applications to . . .   (both from *The Times*, May 1890)

Also available were a Red Hungarian Band and an Anglo-Hungarian Band ('scarlet uniforms')—obviously Hungarian music was 'in' that particular Season. The quality of the music was naturally one of the features by which a dance or reception was judged.

On a higher level, there were the pianists and vocalists who performed at afternoon at-homes and private concerts. These would often be professionals of the highest calibre—even singers currently appearing at Covent Garden—whose names would add cachet to a hostess's function. Some hostesses went in for culture as their 'thing' —sometimes, perhaps, because they really liked it.

Another class of people who must be classified as entertainers were the various grades of tart—from the *corps de ballet* at the variety theatres to the common street-walkers of the Haymarket. They thrived during the Season as at no other time of the year; many a man, after dancing for hours with a succession of pretty girls in low-cut dresses with whom he could not hope for any greater intimacy than a snatched kiss on the stairs or the balcony, must have made his way eastwards in search (not a

Du Maurier,
Punch, *1877*

A SENSITIVE PLANT.   1877.

(Herr Pumpernickel, having just played a Composition of his own, bursts into Tears.)
Chorus of Friends. "OH, WHAT IS THE MATTER? WHAT CAN WE DO FOR YOU?"
Herr Pumpernickel. "ACH! NOSSING! NOSSING! BOT VEN I HEAR REALLY *COOT* MUSIC, ZEN MUST I ALWAYS *VEEP!*"

difficult one) of some 'fair Cyprian' of the night. A young man who lived in London would of course be very likely to have his regular mistress, conveniently maintained in her own lodgings close at hand for whenever he required her company; for those who came to London only for the Season, it was a matter of visiting the restaurants and night-houses in the vicinity of Piccadilly Circus and Regent Street.

SERVANTS

Some of the grander families maintained duplicate establishments in town and country, which meant to some extent employing a second 'set' of servants. The personal staff—lady's maids and valets—would of course attend their mistresses and masters wherever they went; so generally would the butler, the coachman and some of the grooms, the cook, and perhaps others too. But inevitably there would be a certain amount of additional labour involved, for some servants would have to be left behind in the country, and their roles would have to be filled by temporary London staff. In a large house the servants would outnumber the family by several

NO WASTE IN THE KITCHEN.

need occur where Liebig Company's Extract is used. No waste of time, no waste of materials, for with a small quantity of extract, remnants, which by themselves would be insipid and useless, can be made into a delicate soup, or savoury dish.

Get the genuine, signed in Blue,

J. Liebig

LIEBIG
COMPANY'S EXTRACT

Above
Advertisement in ILN, *1899*

REFLECTED GLORY.

Sh--man. "HERE! HI! ARE YOU HIS GRACE THE DUKE OF BAYSWATER?" *Magnificent Flunkey.* "I HAM!"

Right *Du Maurier,* Punch, *1883*

to one; in addition, casual servants would be required when a large reception or ball was being given.

The duties of personal servants during the Season were arduous in the extreme. Ladies and gentlemen needed to change their clothes repeatedly throughout the day as they went from one engagement to the next; a fashionable lady could easily get through six changes of clothes in the course of a single day. On special occasions the preparations would take a good part of the day. Ladies seldom patronised beauty parlours; Madame Rachel of Bond Street drew her clientele from the demi-monde. Hairdressers, too, were seldom patronised, but a lady might send her maid to a hairdressing establishment for instruction when a new hair-style came into vogue. There were, however, hairdressing establishments for gentlemen, conveniently located in Piccadilly, Curzon Street or the St James's Street area.

One must remember that the master–servant relationship was often paternalistic in the best sense of that word. Whatever one's principles on the matter, there is little doubt that in fact the household was often perfectly happy. The Countess of Warwick recalled:

> . . . servants who were as much a part of the household as any member of the family. As far as I know they would as soon have thought of criticising their 'betters' as they would have thought of criticising God. Masters and mistresses were 'different'—a race of favoured beings. It seemed to be a point of honour with that class of servant to cover their employers' misdeeds, and lie for them, and stick by them.

A fashionable lady's preparations. London Magazine, *1904*

My lady in the hands of her maid. London Magazine, *1904*

The butler. Mrs Beeton, *1883*

A good chef—frequently imported from France—was an essential item in any household which prided itself on its entertainment. The standard of cuisine was very high, but was achieved at a horrifying cost. In order to provide meals of the kind quoted in this book, resources comparable to those of a small hotel were required, for not only was there a long list of dishes, but for almost every course a choice was offered, and the chef had to be prepared for the possibility that, once in a while, every single guest would choose the same dish.

The other most important class of servants were those responsible for transport—the coachman and grooms. A big house would possess two or three carriages—a small carriage that the lady of the house might drive herself; a large open victoria

or the like for the leisurely afternoon ride in the Park; and a state carriage for evening use and visits to Buckingham Palace or Marlborough House. In addition, there would be a number of riding horses. Consequently the mews at the back of a big Mayfair house would be a fairly sizeable as well as a very busy place, and the servants would be kept occupied throughout the Season.

Cleaning boots. London Society, *1865*

A merciful custom has been adopted of late years when balls are kept up till 3 or 4 a.m. The hostess arranges with the keeper of a coffee-stall for refreshments of a simple but comfortable kind to be supplied to the coachmen and footmen of her guests, whose long, weary wait outside is thus beguiled of at least one of its disagreeables, hunger.

(Mrs Humphry, *Manners for Women*)

A kindly thought.

SHOPS

Many of the tradespeople of Mayfair and the West End streets must have been largely if not wholly dependent on the trade they did during the three months of the Season. A baker, a butcher or a greengrocer who had the privilege of enjoying the custom of one of the big houses of Park Lane, for instance, would do many times the business in June that he did in December. For them, at least, Lady Dorothy Neville's arguments contain a large element of truth.

Such trade was of course carried on without any knowledge or interference on the part of the lady of the house—the cook would be responsible for ordering whatever was necessary, and though a conscientious wife would keep a watch on bills, she would not have time to get very involved. The back of a big house would be busy all day long with the arrival of tradesmen with their supplies of provisions. One look at the menus and at the variety of ingredients required reveals what quantities of food and drink were consumed by every house in Mayfair, every day of the week, for those three orgiastic months. The power wielded by the kitchen staff responsible for placing the necessary orders was therefore enormous, and some very fancy financial negotiations must have taken place between a cook and his suppliers.

Of the kind of shopping which more directly concerned Society, clothing was far and away the most important. Nearly all clothes were made for the individual; only the most humdrum items were bought ready-made. Every lady's dress was unique, the dictates of fashion being adapted to each individual. The following example is taken at random from *The Ladies' Realm* for the spring of 1897:

> A glimpse of Paris has given us a few hints on what will be seen in London during the next two months. Saque coats, for instance, will not lose favour; these will be worn absurdly short, but will be becoming, owing to their graceful cut and arrangement from the shoulders. Capes will not be so much apparent as these short saque coats, but, if properly cut, they may be donned without any fear of being considered frumpish. In tailor-made gowns, we predict that cord trimmings of rounded-raised designs, mixed with gold and silver, will somewhat take the place of braid. But these adornments will only be found in the ateliers of the best tailors, for their price will be, happily, prohibitive, and the mode will be one that, for some time at least, will not fall into the hands of the vulgar.

A good deal of a lady's time—and if she considered herself 'fashionable', a very great deal of it—was necessarily spent visiting her dressmaker and planning future additions to her wardrobe. This was done in the morning, between 11 a.m. and

Someone Has To Do The Work

A fashionable dressmaker. Living London, *1900*

A Regent Street dress shop, Lewis and Allenby's. London of today, *1890*

ENTICING!

Salesman. "YOU MAY NOT LIKE THE COLOURS, SIR; BUT I ASSURE YOU THEY ARE ALL THE MOST FASHIONABLE SHADES, GUARANTEED TO LAST WELL TOO, FOR I WORE ONE MYSELF ALL LAST SEASON!"

Punch, 1898

Advertisement in Herbert's London Guide, *1883*

2 p.m.; it was not 'done' to go shopping in the afternoon, except in a very casual way. The most fashionable ladies of all went to Paris for their clothes, but the majority made do with English suppliers—all of whom, of course, took their lead from Paris as regards the newest innovations. Princess Alexandra had her clothes from Welborn, in Regent Street, while Worth's was one of the biggest and most expensive establishments. In the West End a lady found all the necessary people to cover every portion of her anatomy with the appropriate garment—dressmakers, tailors, milliners, hatters, corsetiers, hosiers. Most ladies had their 'own' dressmaker, a lady whose creations bore her personal imprint; Madame Kate Reily of Dover Street was perhaps the most famous (and the most expensive), but others were Helen

Metcalfe, Mrs Mason and Miss Viney. Alternatively there were the stores: it was perfectly 'done' for a lady of fashion to patronise the up-and-coming establishments of Marshall and Snelgrove or Debenham and Freebody.

Gentlemen, too, were expected to take their appearance seriously. Like their womenfolk, they had no need to go far to meet their needs—Mayfair and St James provided them with all they required. A man's suit might be made for him by Whitaker of Conduit Street, his shirts (also made for him) by Harborow of Cockspur Street, his boots and shoes (likewise) from Peal's or Lobb's, his hat from Herbert Johnson of Bond Street, his necktie from Welch, Margetson. Thus accoutred, he could hold his own however fashionable his club, however smart his lunch invitations and evening engagements.

145
DRESS JACKET.

146
DRESS COAT,
STEP COLLAR.

147
DRESS COAT,
ROLL COLLAR.

ENTERED AT STATIONER'S HALL.

ILLUSTRATIONS OF BRITISH COSTUMES

EVENING DRESS 1893–4.

Published by The John Williamson Company Limited, 93 & 94 Drury Lane, London, W.C.

OTHER NEEDS

There were all sorts of other people who benefited commercially from the Season: not least the cab drivers, as described by Pascoe:

> The people with the money have gone away. The hansom cabman will soon abate his pride. For months he has put intending fares through a catechism—'Where are they going?' 'Brixton.' 'Oh, that won't suit!' and the lordly cabman drives on in a neat new pair of gloves. With the close of the Season he descends from the perch of pride. Instead of superciliously staring at persons who hail him, *he* hails *them*. He is anxious to be employed, and no longer picks and chooses.

The florists did a roaring trade all Season through. Elaborate floral arrangements were needed for dinner tables and buffets. On the morning of a Drawing Room, hundreds of posy bouquets were despatched by shops like Mrs Green's of Crawford Street, while in the background girls were busy preparing floral masterpieces to stand beside the hostess as she received her guests at the head of some noble staircase.

Another trade which did especially well on Drawing Room days was the photographer's. An establishment like Mayall's of Grafton Street had a continual succession of noble appointments coming on from Buckingham Palace, coping with them at the rate of twelve minutes apiece. Subsequently, those who gave their permission would have their photographs displayed in the windows, along with portraits of the professional beauties and other 'fashionables' of the current Season.

Families which did not maintain their own horses would hire them by the single occasion, by the week or by the entire Season. A typical advertisement ran:

> JOB HORSES—Messrs M. & W. Milton, 6 Park Lane, supply superior High Stepping Pairs and Single Horses of quality, by the month or year.

Carriages of all kinds could be rented in the same way, or one could buy a second-hand carriage, possibly ordered by another family in the previous Season and re-purchased by the maker. A sound second-hand victoria cost in the region of £70.

Caterers were indispensable for the more elaborate parties—no domestic kitchen could cope with the vast quantities of food and drink which were needed, nor could any house muster the necessary staff. Many caterers were at the same time restaurateurs, of course, and thus drew a double benefit from the Season, as did the tea-shops and other purveyors of refreshments. Of Gunter's of Berkeley Square, noted for its ices, Pascoe writes:

> You will see many a coronet on the panels of the carriages drawn up at the railings under the trees; and seated at the little tables of the well-known establishment over the way, many a *grande dame* privileged to wear one.

TEMPORARY BALL ROOMS
Erected in your own Gardens or Enclosures, on Hire for the Evening.
PERFECTLY WARMED, WEATHERPROOF, AND SNOW-RESISTING.
Connected with the House.   *No Need to Remove Furniture.*

PIGGOTT BROS. & COMPANY
57, 58, 59, BISHOPSGATE STREET WITHOUT, LONDON.
ILLUSTRATED HIRE CATALOGUE, WITH FULL PARTICULARS, POST FREE.

For those who battened on Society's self-indulgence, the Season was indeed a very desirable commercial asset. Every step that Society took, every invitation it offered or accepted, every function it attended, meant more money in somebody's pocket. Club servants, fan-makers, menu card-holder makers, crossing-sweepers, theatre-programme sellers, flower-sellers in Piccadilly Circus, cab-touts, wine merchants—all flourished as at no other time of year.

And none more than the printers of visiting cards.

Chapter 13
GOODNIGHT TO
THE SEASON!

The author of these pages has never gone all the way with the dense movement of the British carnival. That is really the word for the period from Easter to midsummer; it is a fine, decorous, expensive, Protestant carnival, in which the masks are not of velvet or silk, but of wonderful deceptive flesh and blood, the material of the most beautiful complexions in the world. Holding that the great interest of London is the sense the place gives us of multitudinous life, it is doubtless an inconsequence not to care most for the phase of greatest intensity. But there is life and life, and the rush and crush of these weeks of fashion is after all but a tolerably mechanical expression of human forces. It goes without saying that it is a more universal, brilliant, spectacular one than can be seen anywhere else; and it is not a defect that these forces often take the form of very beautiful women. I risk the declaration that the London Season brings together, year by year, an unequalled collection of handsome persons . . .

There are moments when one can almost forgive the follies of June for the sake of the smile which the sceptical old city puts on for the time. Most perhaps does she seem to smile at the end of the summer days, when the light lingers and lingers, though the shadows lengthen and the mists redden and the belated riders, with dinners to dress for, hurry away from the trampled arena of the Park. The population, at that hour, moves mainly westward, and sees the dust of the long day's racket turned into a dull golden haze. There is something that has doubtless often, at this particular moment, touched the fancy even of the bored and the blasé, in such an emanation of hospitality, of waiting dinners, of the festal idea, and the whole spectacle of the West End preparing herself for an evening six parties deep. The scale on which she entertains is stupendous, and her invitations and 'reminders' are as thick as the leaves of the forest.

For half an hour, in the region of 8 o'clock, every hurrying vehicle contains an obvious diner-out. To consider only the rattling hansoms, the white neckties and 'dressed' heads which greet you from over the apron, in a quick, interminable succession, conveys an overwhelming impression of a complicated world. Who are they all, and where are they all going, and whence have they come, and what smoking kitchens and gaping portals and marshalled flunkeys are prepared to receive them? There are broughams standing at every door, and carpets laid down for the footfall of the issuing, if not the entering, reveller. The pavements are empty now, in the fading light, in the big dusty squares and the stuccoed streets of gentility, save for the groups of small children, holding others that are smaller—Ameliar-Ann entrusted with Sarah Jane—who collect, wherever the strip of carpet lies, to see the fine ladies pass from the carriage or the house. The West End is dotted with these pathetic little gazing groups; it is the party of the poor—*their* Season.
(Henry James, in *The Century Magazine*, 1888)

The Party That Lasted 100 Days

Without our American commentators—Henry James and Richard Harding Davis and the anonymous contributors of *Harpers Magazine*—the task of reconstructing the London Season would be very much more difficult, particularly if one wishes to catch the unmistakeable flavour which can derive only from first-hand accounts rendered by those who have themselves participated in the ritual goings-on. American visitors to London provide us with the finest witnesses: first, because they had to spell out for the benefit of their distant readers things that native commentators would have taken for granted; and secondly, because while sufficiently respectful of the affair to describe it with sympathy, they never failed to retain their sense of humour and proportion. Even while they admired, they never lost sight of the ultimate absurdity of the business.

Their stance, surely, must be that of the intelligent onlooker from a century later. 'It's foolish but it's fun!' could hardly be improved upon as an epitaph for the London Season. Today we have learned to be more socially conscientious; few of us would dare to approve anything so blatantly anti-egalitarian. And yet it would be petty—and foolish—to deny at least a little sympathy to those relics of a past age, who did their best to hang on to the old way of life when over their heads resounded the pick-axes and sledge-hammers that were changing the world about them.

When one thinks about the gentlemen and ladies who took part in the Season,

Piccadilly in 1900, Living London

WEARER AND MAKER.

From Cassells,'
1884

WEALTHY, and young, and fair,
　　With the sun's own gold in her shining hair,
　　With the coral's rose-dye on cheeks and lips,
　　And eyes whose blue radiance finds eclipse
In lashes of ebon darkness ; around,
Rich Parian mirrors that touch the ground
Reflect her every charm—
From her graceful head to her tiny feet,
Dimpled shoulder and rounded arm,
Perfectly splendid and complete.
On the lace-hung table before her, lie
Flowers and perfumes, and jewellery,
In dainty cases of opal and gold,
Rare as the delicate treasures they hold.
Diamonds gleam 'midst her tresses, bright
As stars in the evening's golden light ;
Robed in white satin that, fold upon fold,
Floats round her like moonbeams—as pure and cold ;
Ready with murmur, with glance, and with smile,
The heart to wreck and the soul to beguile.
Each night for feasting, each morning for play—
The rich robes hide bravely the feet of clay !

after vicariously working one's way along with them from Stanhope Gate to Goodwood, one's overwhelming sensation is of isolation. They themselves would have used the word 'exclusive'; they thought they were keeping the rest of the world out of their sanctuary. But as one looks back at them now, it seems rather the other way round. They were shutting themselves off from the real world, playing their own little games in their own private playground; they were children, even the most exalted and be-titled of them—children with too much pocket money. And then we remind ourselves that they weren't children at all, they were rich and powerful people—the richest and most powerful in the land. They owned the land itself and most of the buildings erected on it, they owned the great institutions of the country, they framed its laws and dictated its policies, they were looked up to and respected and deferred to by the rest of the populace.

Those who ventured to criticise them were a tiny minority, less rich and infinitely less powerful. On their own, the critics could never have destroyed the old regime, for there were too many people anxious and eager to bolster it up, bringing in new wealth and power in return for the privilege of being permitted to join the club.

It is often said that it was the First World War which finally demolished Society. But the war was only the *coup de grâce*: Society was already crumbling fast as H. G. Wells's new middle classes gathered strength and purpose. Society had no sense of purpose to unite it: individuals might move with the times, carry out reforms, adopt new attitudes, but Society as a whole was dedicated to preserving the status quo, and this negative aim was all that bound it together.

Nothing expresses this better than the judgment passed in the 1920s by Frances, Countess of Warwick, looking back to the 1880s and 1890s when she had been one of Society's most dazzling stars:

> Just before her death, Lady Paget, one of the most indefatigable hostesses of her time, was driving with me down what was patently a changed Piccadilly. With an upward glance at the bow windows of the Turf Club, whence no longer the male rank and fashion of the eighties and nineties looked out in criticism at the passing carriages and their fair occupants, Lady Paget laid a hand on my arm and said, 'How glad I am that you and I lived in and experienced the wonderful times for ever gone!'
>
> Whether or not I reciprocated that sentiment at the time does not matter. Today I should certainly demur. The present times are to me incomparably more absorbing. Life is in reality more spacious than before, though individual wealth is passing from the control of the few, and for women at any rate a new era has dawned. To the girl of today I would say, 'Don't believe grandmother's tales of her unattainable conquests. You are healthier, saner, more alert than she ever was or could hope to be . . .'
>
> Society in my youth walked like sheep. Had Lady Paget lived in the present day, it is pretty certain that she would have found some outlet for her abounding vitality other than the round of frivolous engagements and entertaining which formed such a large part of social life in England in the eighties and nineties . . . I find consolation in the fact that there are other interests to cultivate than are to be found in the butterfly life of a Society queen.
>
> (*Life's Ebb and Flow*, 1929)

Goodnight To The Season

Goodnight to the Season!—the dances,
The filling of hot little rooms,
The glancing of rapturous glances,
The fancyings of fancy costumes;
The pleasures which fashion makes duties,
The praising of fiddles and flutes,
The luxury of looking at Beauties,
The tedium of talking to mutes;
The female diplomatists, planners
Of matches for Laura and Jane;
The ice of her Ladyship's manners,
The ice of his Lordship's champagne.

Goodnight to the Season!—Another
Will come, with its trifles and toys,
And hurry away, like its brother,
In sunshine, and odour, and noise.
Will it come with a rose or a briar?
Will it come with a blessing or curse?
Will its bonnets be lower or higher?
Will its morals be better or worse?
Will it find me grown thinner or fatter,
Or fonder of wrong or of right?
Or married—or buried?—no matter:
Goodnight to the Season—goodnight!
                    (Winthrop Mackworth Praed)

*The morning
after the party.*
Graphic, *1875*

Books Consulted

Finding material for a study of this sort is largely a matter of accident. Nobody could fight single-handed through the accumulated periodical literature of the period, nobody could even skim all the memoirs and autobiographies which might contain useful material. After a while, one finds that some accounts merely repeat and confirm what others have said; at which point one can be tolerably certain that a reasonably authentic picture has been built up. It would be possible, I am sure, to duplicate my study without using any of the sources I consulted; if I list some of them, it is to indicate the *type* of source, rather than to suggest that these are the only authorities, or even necessarily the best.

PERSONAL VIEWS

Sara Jeanette Duncan, *An American Girl in London* (1891).
Douglas Jerrold and Gustave Doré, *London, a Pilgrimage* (1872).
Robert Machray, *The Night Side of London* (1902).
The Duke of Manchester, *My Candid Recollections* (1932).
Lady Dorothy Neville, *Under Five Reigns* (1910).
Charles Eyre Pascoe, *London of Today* (1890 and 1903 editions).
Hippolyte Taine, *Notes on England* (1872).
Frances, Countess of Warwick, *Life's Ebb and Flow* (1929).
Montagu Williams, *Round London* (1892).

ETIQUETTE BOOKS

'A Member of the Aristocracy', *Manners and Rules of Good Society* (1887).
Lady Colin Campbell, *The Etiquette of Good Society* (1894).
G. R. M. Devereux, *Etiquette for Men* (no date).
——*Etiquette for Women* (no date).
Mrs Humphry, *Manners for Men* (no date).
——*Manners for Women* (no date).

JOURNALS

The Century Magazine (New York).
The Graphic.
Harmsworth's London Magazine.
Harpers Magazine (New York).
The Illustrated London News.
The Ladies' Realm.
The Pall Mall Magazine.
The Times.

Index